Merrily's Border

Merrily's Border

by
Phil Rickman

with photographs by
John Mason

Logaston Press

LOGASTON PRESS
Little Logaston Woonton Almeley
Herefordshire HR3 6QH
www.logastonpress.co.uk

Published by Logaston Press 2009
Copyright text © Phil Rickman 2009
www.philrickman.co.uk
Copyright illustrations © as acknowledged pages 99-100 2009

ISBN 978 1 906663 16 2 (Hardback)
978 1 906663 17 9 (Paperback)

Typeset by Logaston Press
and printed and bound in Poland
www.polskabook.pl

Front cover photograph: Wern Derys (John Mason)
Back cover photographs: Radnor Plain (John Mason),
Weobley (Logaston Press)
Hardback jacket flaps: Cascob Church (front) (John Mason)
Queen Stone (back) (John Mason)

Contents

Note

This book is a result of all the letters and emails which come in daily from readers who say how *real* the Merrily Watkins series feels.

I can't claim too much of the credit for that. As John Mason's pictures demonstrate, virtually all the locations are real, even if some smaller communities are protected by fictional names. And so is much of the background: actual history, legend, folklore and customs, overlaid by recent and current issues.

Essentially, this is a guide to some of the more mysterious elements along the mid and southern Welsh Border. Researching the novels takes me into some areas which seem never to have been fully explored before — certainly not in fiction. You might also find material here which has never appeared in a guide book either. What happens ... putting together a novel, you find yourself drawing together disparate threads, and then, suddenly, you're looking at a whole new tapestry.

As you can imagine, it's quite difficult to make a book like this work without giving away key elements of the fictional plots, but I've tried not to reveal details which might spoil anything for new readers of the novels. To avoid any of those *look away now* moments, information is, just occasionally, incomplete ... although, where possible, other sources are indicated for readers who want to know more.

A lot of people are due thanks for help putting together these stories, and most are credited in various novels. Ced Jackson and Richard Bartholomew, of the British Society of Dowsers, provided extra information for this book, along with various deliverance consultants and ministers, some named, some preferring not to be. Thanks, finally, to Andy & Karen Johnson of Logaston Press for the extra pictures, classy page layouts ... and the detrmination to get it right.

Phil Rickman

Introduction

A Border Thing

Borders. For as long as I can remember I've been drawn to them, this one in particular. Borders are risky places, where the unexpected happens. As a kid in Lancashire, an hour or so's drive from Wales, I used to fantasize about what it would be like living on the border. *Right* on the border. One foot in England, one foot in Wales — how would that *feel*?

That was before I'd learned of the very real mystique around borders, the suggestion that a geographical frontier might also be the division between different states of mind, different ways of thinking ... even (careful, now ...) different levels of existence.

Anyway, for most of my adult life, I've lived very close either to the Welsh border or the English border, depending on your standpoint, passing almost daily between the two nations, in an area which is superficially serene but still smouldering with history and clouded with folklore. And now I'm writing novels exploring its textures: a series of novels which seem to have created their own fictional genre: mysteries with more than one layer of mystery.

Mysteries — or so I like to think — in the original sense. The Merrily novels are a combination of the crime thriller and the possibilities of *something else*. Even today, surprisingly few people, locals or incomers, scorn belief in the paranormal. They'll smile sometimes, but they won't scoff.

The series is centred on Herefordshire, extending into Radnor Forest, the hills of Shropshire and Monmouthshire, the Black Mountains and the Malverns. The history and legends of each location tend to invade the stories, along with current issues, and in the end I'm always surprised at how little needs to be made up.

This is a fringe area, in many ways neither England nor Wales, always thinly populated and thus largely ignored by national and regional media. It's always had secrets and usually been able to keep them. The Welsh leader, Owain Glyndwr was last heard of not in the mountains of north Wales but in the Golden Valley of Herefordshire. Salman Rushdie, under Islamic death-sentence, was successfully hidden near Brecon. It's even been rumoured that Lord Lucan, on the run after the murder of his children's nanny, found temporary shelter on the edge of Offa's Dyke before leaving the country.

Less furtively, there was Arthur Conan Doyle tracking the Hound of the Baskervilles, Edward Elgar on his bike, Alfred Watkins sighting ancient tracks between standing stones and steeples.

Today, rock stars and royals find sanctuary here. That famous face you think you saw in Leominster or somewhere ... well, it probably was. This is a safe haven for the famous and the notorious — nobody gets too excited. As my friend Gomer Parry once said, 'En't a problem for us, boy. Long as they don't get too cosy with the sheep.'

Gomer Parry. In many ways, this man *is* the Border. Old but ageless, built like a thorn tree on a hillside facing the west wind, Gomer has hair like a battered lavatory brush, wears thick glasses, smokes roll-ups. Raised in upland, subsistence farming, Gomer decided — long before it became a Government buzz-word — that it was time to diversify.

So he went into Plant Hire. Bought himself a secondhand JCB with which to dig field drains and soakaways for septic tanks. It gave him a certain status, the freedom of the countryside and the ability to crush lesser vehicles with one swing of the bucket. Also a good living because, as he often points out, fields is always gonner need draining and if your soakaway don't soak away you're in deep ... trouble.

Gomer was born in old Radnorshire, at the time the least-known and least-populated county in southern Britain. When my wife, Carol and I were working there as journalists we encountered him — memorably

— several times. He's an independent man who observes the natural laws of the countryside and the rules of Plant Hire — digger chivalry. Most of the time he hates the council, the Government and particularly the shiny-arsed townies who run DEFRA (young Jane Watkins says it stands for Destroying Every Farm-reared Animal — Gomer likes that).

It took me a while to get to know Gomer, and it was a few years before I felt qualified to write about him, having observed his basic rule for survival on the Border: keep real quiet till you knows the score.

Surprising how many people get that one wrong and wind up face-down in the ole slurry pit.

The first Merrily Watkins novel, *The Wine of Angels*, was to have been a Gomer Parry novel until a pivotal aspect of the plot made it necessary for the village of Ledwardine to have a woman vicar.

After which, Merrily, in her insecure, self-effacing, less-than-confident way, took over.

In the next novel, *Midwinter of the Spirit*, she was appointed diocesan exorcist for Hereford and became a series. Now, if you Google exorcism/Hereford in the hope of finding someone to help you over some domestic intrusion you can't rationally explain, I'm afraid you're likely to be directed, at some stage, to Merrily Watkins.

She's embarrassed, of course. Merrily isn't into fame or the cult-of-personality. This wasn't at all what she had in mind when she arrived in the village of Ledwardine as a thirty-something widow with a slightly resentful teenage daughter, Jane, who at first didn't want to be here and definitely didn't want her mum to be a vicar, not least because her own spiritual leanings were distinctly pagan.

To to be honest, I never imagined anyone could write a whole series of fairly dark crime novels from the point of view of a country vicar, female or male. I had no idea, back then, that she was going to turn, quite rapidly, into the best idea I'd ever had.

RADNORSHIRE

SHROPSHIRE

Leintwardine • Ludlow

River Lugg

Cascob
Discoed.
Ednol
Llandegley
Tomen Castle
Castell Crugeryr
Four Stones
Old Radnor
Pembridge
Eardisland • Leominster

River Arrow
Kington
Dilwyn
Weobley
Ss Cosmas & Damian
Stretford

Bromyard •

WORCESTERSHIRE

Avenbury
Castle Frome
FROME VALLEY
Great Malvern
Malvern Hills

Kinnersley

HEREFORDSHIRE

Arthur's Stone

Credenhill

Rotherwas
HEREFORD
Dinedor

Ledbury
Hereford Beacon
Whiteleafed Oak

• Wern Derys

Much Marcle •
• Kempley

Black Mountains

Abbey Dore •
• Kilpeck
Llanwarne

• Site of Ariconium
• Ross-on-Wye

BRECONSHIRE

• Garway
COUGHTON VALLEY

GLOUCESTERSHIRE

Queen Stone •

Monmouth

Forest of Dean

1   Old Cider

Twisty old devil.
Looked as if it held a grudge in every scabby branch, and
it wouldn't give you any fruit, on principle. because, left to
rot, apple trees ...
                              ... they grows resentful.
Merrily's grandad had told her that once, when she was a little
girl. Frightening her ...

The Wine of Angels

Like most vicars, Merrily is from Off. She has ancestry in the area, but did her training in Liverpool. She's a thirty-something widow with a teenage daughter. She smokes. When she drops something on her foot she doesn't say, 'Oh, bother'. And, no, she *doesn't* look like Dawn French.

Bringing in a stranger is always a useful device for a novelist. After all, most of the readers are also going to be from Off, so viewing an area through the eyes of an outsider lets you dwell on its eccentricities, highlighting both appealing blemishes and sinister stains which locals might no longer notice.

The village of Ledwardine is the missing location on the Herefordshire Black and White Trail. Think timber-framing and white plaster. Think Pembridge, Weobley, Dilwyn, Eardisland; Ledwardine has bits of all of them. It used to be a working village, sustained by farming and the cider industry, but its current prosperity is largely a result of its olde worlde appeal. Here's what it says on a notorious website sponsored by estate agents keen to persuade wealthy folk from Off to move in.

LEDWARDINE

Once known as The Village in the Orchard, this community may have begun as simply that. The old centre of the village is still partly enclosed by the remains of an apple orchard dating back at least to medieval times, as do some of its black and white timber-framed houses. Earlier settlement is suggested by recent archaeological discoveries at the foot of Cole Hill, whose Iron Age fortifications are a reminder of a turbulent past. Today, Ledwardine ('Jewel of The New Cotswolds' — *Daily Telegraph*) is serene and inviting. The cobbled village square, with its small, open market-hall supported by oak pillars, is enlivened by a variety of retail outlets, including a bookshop, gallery and delicatessen, as well as the 15th-century Black Swan Inn, noted for its fine food.

FACILITIES: the village, although largely self-sufficient, is a mere ten minute drive from the nearest town of Leominster and no more than twenty-five minutes from the progressive cathedral city of Hereford, now undergoing extensive commercial renewal. Several highly reputable private schools are within easy reach.

LEDWARDINE STAR-RATING **** *and rising!*

WE SAY: *buy now*, while prices are competitive and this area is still relatively obscure.

Note the orchard, central to *The Wine of Angels* and, nine books later, *To Dream of the Dead*. Like many apparently-innocuous features of the border, it's more than it seems. When Merrily arrives in Ledwardine, as priest-in-charge, there's blood on the apple trees and more trouble to come. Incomers to Ledwardine are promoting a summer festival designed to raise the village's prominence on the tourist map and revive the traditional local cider. Meanwhile, the truth is about to be uncovered about a 17th-century vicar accused of witchcraft. Then a teenage girl goes missing — and not the first.

This book is full of apples. Apples and cider, apples and murder, apples and the unseen. For example, as the old folklorist Lucy Devenish explains to Jane Watkins, if you cut an apple crossways — that is, not through the stalk — you'll find ...

'There.' She held out a half in the palm of each hand. 'What do you see?'

Jane leaned over the counter. The green-white pulp was veined with thin green lines and dots which made a kind of wheel.

'Count the spokes,' Lucy said.

'Five.'

'It makes a five-pointed star, you see? Inside a circle. A pentagram ... a very ancient symbol of purification and protection. And there's one at the heart of every apple. That says something, doesn't it?'

Lucy Devenish runs a small, crowded shop called Ledwardine Lore, which provides exactly what it says on the sign. Lucy knows more than anybody about the village's secrets, many of which relate to ...

Cider

Which, in Herefordshire, goes back, almost certainly, to pre-Roman times, although the Romans apparently preferred perry (the equivalent, made from pears). It's been in and out of fashion ever since, always popular with farmworkers, occasionally favoured by the gentry, especially in the 18th century. There are still said to be nearly ten thousand acres of cider orchard in the county. Several independent cider companies are still based there, while Hereford's best-known cider firm, Bulmers, has changed hands twice recently, with owners from Off replaced by owners from seriously Off. You can find out how the wine of angels was originally made in the cider museum by the side of Sainsbury's. A shadowy place with the dense musky atmosphere I wanted the novel to carry.

I've always enjoyed discovering a weird underside to familiar items: the poisoned apple, the worm in the apple, so it was good to find someone of a similar mind, even if long dead. Much of the folklore in this novel and several of the others was plucked from the pages of an invaluable book by

Ella Mary Leather

Published in 1912, Mrs Leather's *The Folklore of Herefordshire* may be the best collection of local legends and traditions ever published in Britain. At least, I've never found one more detailed. This inquisitive Victorian lady (born 1874) hung out with gypsies and old farmworkers and burrowed deep into the red border soil to uncover half-buried pagan roots, customs, traditions, superstitions, folk tales, folk song ...

the rhythm and pulse of the Border.

'No record in cold print can give the reader an idea of the pleasure experienced in collecting the elusive material we call folk lore from the living brains of men and women of whose lives it has formed an integral part,' she writes in her preface, after relating how it all began with Martha B—

> ... a tiny, dark-haired, olive skinned woman who, when I first remembered her, gathered apples in a Herefordshire orchard ... Martha smoked a little clay pipe, apologetically 'by doctor's orders'; her greeting was always 'Good day, missie, God bless you'; I learned that this formula was an infallible protection against witchcraft and the evil eye. It was Martha who could tell how the house which once stood in the wood had been pulled down because it was so badly haunted; she herself saw ghosts and could point out the very spots where they appeared to her.

Mrs Leather was from Weobley, a place very close to Ledwardine. If she'd been born 50 years later, she would almost certainly have been Lucy Devenish's best friend.

The only book to pick up Mrs Leather's trail in recent years is Roy Palmer's *Herefordshire Folklore*, part of his valuable and timely series, which also deals with Radnorshire, Shropshire, Monmouthshire and Worcestershire. Arguably, still the most mysterious area of southern Britain.

On the advice of Ella Mary, I called the original Ledwardine cider apple the *Pharisees Red* — the *pharisees* a corruption of *farises*, an archaic local word for fairies, whose tiny lights, according to legend, may be seen in the Ledwardine orchard, along with bits of old Edgar Powell, who blows his head off with a 12-bore shotgun during an attempted revival of

Wassailing

This is a custom usually carried out on Twelfth Night in an attempt to ensure a good crop of apples the following autumn. It's been revived in Herefordshire over the past twenty years, with wassails in Much

Marcle in the east and Eardisley in the west. In can involve pouring cider over the roots of an apple tree or, as in *The Wine of Angels*, firing shotguns through the branches after an appropriately encouraging chant.

The Twelfth Night ceremonies may have begun with the lighting of fires in wheat fields to encourage healthy crops. The lighting up of the darkest time of the year. The pagan origins are clear. Mrs Leather also describes a ritual I just had to borrow, which seems to get inside the earth itself.

> The men stand in a ring around the fire and 'holloa auld cider'. They sing on one very deep note, very slowly, holding each syllable as long as possible, 'Auld—Ci—der.' The 'der' becomes a sort of growl at the end and is an octave below the first two notes; it has a weird dirge-like effect.

The title of this novel comes from the line 'Tears are the wine of angels, the best ... to quench the devil's fires' attributed to a 17th-century Herefordshire poet and mystic whose work is often quoted in the book to echo certain themes.

Thomas Traherne (1637-1674)

The son of a Hereford shoemaker, Traherne became Rector of Credenhill several centuries before the SAS moved in. Lucy Devenish was not the only person to have detected elements of paganism or at least pantheism in his poetry.

Essentially, Traherne was a pre-hippy advocate of happiness ... *felicity*. He knew and loved the countryside in all its jewelled moods. His philosophy was, *God gave it to you — enjoy*. In fact, he suggested, *not* enjoying it was an insult to creation, and his lines,

> You never enjoy the world aright
> Till the sea itself floweth in your veins
> Till you are clothed in the heavens
> And crowned with the stars

were memorably set to music, at the zenith of psychedelia, by Mike Heron of The Incredible String Band, who clearly held similar views.

In *The Wine of Angels*, Lucy Devenish introduces Traherne's poems to Lol Robinson, a songwriter and musician who gets closer, with almost every book, to Merrily Watkins. Lol's career in folk-rock, with the band Hazey Jane, was cut short in difficult circumstances. He finds himself relating increasingly to the artist who influenced his earliest songs and provided the band with its name:

Nick Drake (1948-1974)

Lol is one of the many contemporary singer-songwriters influenced to the point of minor obsession by someone far more famous now than he ever was in his brief lifetime. In a way, Lol, though more than twenty years younger, is what Nick Drake might have become if he'd survived.

Nick's songs, like *Way to Blue*, *Hazey Jane II*, *River Man*, *From the Morning*, convey a unique sense of wistful, pastoral Englishness. The problem at the time of their release was that there were just so many ground-breaking albums around that it was easy for something this subtle and restrained to fall through the cracks.

The albums had poor sales. It didn't help that Nick himself was becoming increasingly withdrawn and had problems facing an audience. Someone who went to one of his very rare concerts told me he'd physically half-turn himself away from the crowd.

Eventually, it became clear that Nick was becoming mentally ill. He died at his parents' home in Tanworth-in-Arden, Warwickshire, from an overdose of anti-depressants which may or may not have been accidental. You can hear the chill of despair in his later songs, in the elemental menace of *Pink Moon* and the raw bleakness of *Black Eyed Dog*.

It wasn't until the mid-1990s that Nick's three albums, *Five Leaves Left*, *Bryter Layter* and *Pink Moon*, took off, artists including Paul Weller and Beth Orton having identified him as a major influence. In 2007, after many bootlegs, his early home-recordings, which included his mother Molly's own surprisingly effective songs, were finally released as the album *Family Tree*, with sleeve-notes (and a duet on the sadly prophetic cover of *All My Trials, Soon Be Over*) by his sister, the actress Gabrielle Drake.

Around the time of *Family Tree*, I finally went to Tanworth-in-Arden. As did Lol Robinson, in the ninth novel, *The Fabric of Sin*.

Nick shares with his parents, Molly and Rodney, a modest stone under an oak tree in the raised churchyard at Tanworth. It's a lovely spot which will always, for me, carry a soundtrack of *From the Morning*, the soft, summery final song on the final album. For Lol, inevitably, it was more compli-

cated and, with the help of Gabrielle Drake and Cally, who handles Nick's business affairs, we were able to catch the moment on the abridged audio book of *Fabsin*. Lol's own collection, 'Songs from Lucy's Cottage', is available as a CD — details on the website www.philrickman.co.uk.

Meanwhile, back in *The Wine of Angels*, Merrily is faced with a series of inexplicable and possibly paranormal events in and around the 17th-century crookedly timber-framed vicarage where she and Jane live. She tries to elicit some advice from her employers on how to deal with them, only to find that the Church of England tends to consider the idea of psychic phenomena slightly embarrassing. Slowly, Merrily finds out who her friends are: Lucy Devenish, the folklorist, Lol Robinson, the songwriter, and Gomer Parry who, in semi-retirement from Plant Hire, digs the graves and looks after the churchyard.

It isn't until the second book, *Midwinter of the Spirit*, that Merrily becomes aware of the Deliverance ministry, the Church's secret service.

2   Something a bit dark

After *Wine* I couldn't bring myself to dump Merrily. Or Jane. Particularly Jane. But I definitely didn't want to write a series of what are known in the USA as 'clerical mysteries' in which persons of the cloth implausibly investigate cosy murders. If Merrily was to survive, she had to be authentically employed in some area of the job which might realistically involve her with criminal behaviour and the underside of spirituality.

The answer appeared to lie in Deliverance. Or, as it was previously known, exorcism — the name having been changed, in the Anglican church, as a result of a horrifyingly frenzied murder.

In 1974, just a year after shocking scenes of demonic possession in the film *The Exorcist* had led to medical alerts in cinemas all over Britain, a 31-year-old unemployed handyman called Michael Taylor, from Ossett, near Barnsley, went to a local minister, claiming to be possessed by devils. Two priests subsequently embarked on an all-night exorcism, after which they told him they'd cast out an estimated forty demons.

Taylor then went home and savagely killed his wife, tearing out her eyes and her tongue.

Within the Church of England, this had repercussions at the highest level. The Archbishop of Canterbury at the time, Donald Coggan, said, 'We must get this business out of the mumbo-jumbo of magic. I think there are many cases where the more rash exorcists have bypassed the work of psychiatrists.'

New rules and new guidelines for exorcists were introduced — followed, twelve years later, by the official casting-out of the term exorcism. Henceforth, each diocese would have a Deliverance adviser, whose own advisers should include a psychiatrist. The new watchword was caution, and it still is.

A former deliverance minister in Herefordshire said, 'I always remember my predecessor saying to me, "This is a mucky world and you come across mucky things. It's not a very nice job. You get a sense of something a bit dark." He was right. You do find strange circumstances and disturbed people. You can actually feel the hairs going up on the back of your neck even while you're looking for the rational explanations.'

Because of increasing demand and the need, these days, always to cover your back, one deliverance minister per diocese is often seen as insufficient. Now it tends to be a team, whose main function is to offer advice and support to local priests faced with aspects of the unexplained in their parishes.

In a big diocese there could be twelve people involved, including psychiatrists. Which means there are now more trained exorcists working in the UK than at any time in the history of the Church ... and this in a so-called secular age.

'We are, in a way, getting more medieval with every year that passes,' says Canon Michael Wadsworth, for some years a member of a deliverance team based at Ely in the Cambridgeshire Fens. 'There's a sense in which secular men and woman tend to believe a lot more — things their grandparents would have thought rubbish. And the difference now is that people want to do something about it.'

I've learned a lot about the procedures and the pitfalls of exorcism in the ten years since the Merrily Watkins series began. From the start, I wanted the stories to be absolutely authentic. No gratuitous horror, no hint of fantasy ... and a central character who is flawed, paranoid and doesn't always get it right.

At first, the clergy I approached for background information were understandably suspicious. Then, after the second novel, a deliverance minister — someone I didn't, at the time, know — emailed to say he thought the low-key approach and the balance between the real and the imagined were 'exactly right'. As other approving emails filtered through from what's regarded as the coal-face of Christianity, I learned a lot ... and realised that Merrily, with her nicotine habit, her uncertainty and her occasional lapses into language not found in prayer books, wasn't exactly the maverick I'd initially had in mind. Closer, in fact, to the norm.

Deliverance is the Church's secret service, often regarded with suspicion within the C of E, in much the same way as the police mistrust the spooks of Special Branch. Some image-conscious senior clerics see it as a potentially dangerous throwback to the days of the Witchfinder General.

Which may be why deliverance ministers are usually hand-picked by their bishops. Like Merrily, they were often reluctant to take on a role which involves dealing with both human delusion and — even worse — the possibility that some of it *isn't* delusion.

The priests who actually volunteer for deliverance work, in the hope of a hand-to-hand scrap with the powers of evil, are the ones considered least suitable for the job. What the Church is looking for, it seems, is a quality of restraint. And, when you need to separate the real from the imagined, a touch of scepticism is also helpful.

'Someone who says "I need to be exorcized" is usually someone looking for an easy answer,' one exorcist told me, and someone who should be handled with protective gloves. But if even alleged spiritual invasion of a person is rare, property is more vulnerable. It's mainly about ghosts.

The two most commonly reported phenomena encountered by the deliverance ministry are poltergeists and what have become known as 'bereavement apparitions' — sightings, usually by close relatives, of the newly-dead.

It's been estimated that one in four bereaved relatives — husbands and wives, sons and daughters — or even work colleagues will catch occasional glimpses of the departed in familiar spots. A deliverance co-ordinator in Herefordshire says it can sometimes become contagious.

'While many will have some hazy experiences of seeing or hearing the person who has died — which will cease — for a few, these continue and become very vivid, especially if the death was unexpected or complicated. Other people close to the bereaved person may come to share these experiences and reinforce the problem of being unable to let go of the dead person.'

This might be treated by an explanatory chat over a cup of tea, and perhaps prayers or, in extreme cases, a Requiem Eucharist — in effect a second funeral service.

But what are we talking about here? Is it an actual ghost or what psychiatrists would call a psychological projection?

The current co-chairman of British exorcism's governing body, the Christian Deliverance Study Group, is the Bishop of Monmouth, Dominic Walker, perhaps Britain's most experienced exorcist.

Bishop Dominic comes across as urbane, laid-back and well practised in the art of understatement. He says he believes that ninety per cent of all apparitions are mental projections, and it takes some prompting to get him to talk about the time he believes he actually stood next to one.

A ghost, that is. A *real* ghost.

A family had moved into a house to find that the upstairs was already occupied by a middle-aged woman with one leg who would appear and then vanish before their eyes. It emerged that a woman had, in fact, committed suicide there not long after having a leg amputated.

Dominic Walker decided to assemble the family for a Requiem Eucharist — a communion service or Anglican mass for the repose of the dead — in the bedroom where the woman had died, using a dressing table as an altar. Contrary to popular belief, ghosts are not actually exorcised in the *get thee hence* sense; the aim is to direct them towards eternal peace.

'And as we were celebrating the mass, she appeared,' the Bishop recalled. 'It wasn't a frightening experience. It just looked as if we'd been joined by someone else, and that person had only one leg. I thought, Either this is *my* psychological projection or I've been set up. It was only at the end of the service that members of the family said to me, Do you know that when you were praying for her she appeared?'

The woman, he says, finally vanished, never to return.

But it isn't always so easy. Sometimes it takes repeated Requiems and aftercare. A woman minister told me of a case where an apparent poltergeist turned into something out of Hitchcock's Psycho — a man attacked in the shower looked down to find blood issuing from a cut in his leg.

Strange, angelic figures appear in a picture I took at Garway

'I told the couple I wanted to say prayers in the house and then blessed water and salt and blessed each room. Which was fine till I reached the landing between the bedroom and bathroom.

'The back of my neck was crawling, and I felt cold but there was no draught, and I realised how hard it was getting to say the prayer I wanted to say. I had to concentrate to get my mouth to make the words. It was like I could hear them in my head, but something was stopping me from forming them.

'And I felt threatened, like something was trying to force me to stop. I was actually quite scared of what would happen. I could feel something surrounding me. I guess it felt like it would attack if it could, but as long as I kept saying the words, it couldn't. But saying the words was so hard.

'With hindsight, I think that there was a fight-back on that landing. I was aware of an anger, rage even. Mostly I just get aware of whatever it is, but no real fight. The house is free of problems now, anyway.'

Canon Michael Wadsworth recalls going with another priest to help a colleague suffering psychic persecution in his own vicarage.

'Ornaments — some quite heavy — were moving, often in the middle of the night. He was distraught — at the end of his tether. There was definitely a malign influence — a troubled spirit.

'We conducted a Requiem Eucharist and opened every window and every door — it was a fine summer's day. While we worked inside the house, he went outside and shouted at the top of his voice, "Do your bloody worst!"'

Apparently, it worked.

What was perhaps Michael Wadsworth's most curious case involved a very old prayer book given as a legacy to his church. It had belonged to a priest and went into general use.

'It was interesting how, in at least two homes belonging to people who attended the church and used that particular prayer book, things started to happen — poltergeist phenomena and voices. I didn't tell people, just ceased to use the prayer book and blessed it, privately. And it stopped.

'I'm probably being whimsical about it, but being in my job makes you like this. I've come away with the lifetime motto: there's no such thing as a gratuitous coincidence. Sometimes it seems as if we're trembling on the brink of the absurd, but religion is like that.'

If all this has made it seem relatively easy — a splash of holy water, a well-timed ritual and, even if there's a struggle, the good guys always win — it's important to point out that it *doesn't* always work. Most deliverance ministers have painful ongoing cases they can't discuss because the victims would be identified.

There are apparent presences which repeated Requiem eucharists have failed to erase. There are cases where parish priests have suffered breakdowns or even quit the ministry. Most deliverance ministers will tell you they've watched objects move or at least felt the intense cold, a cold you experience inside as a kind of frigid void. The borderline between psychiatric illness and what one senior exorcist calls psychic or demonic *oppression* is continually blurred.

In *Midwinter of the Spirit*, a new bishop of Hereford, having heard of Merrily's problems in *The Wine of Angels*, invites her to take on the additional job of deliverance consultant for the diocese.

Consultant is an appropriate word, as the diocesan exorcist is mostly there to advise. If you have a problem, you normally take it to the local vicar or rector who may then refer it to the deliverance minister.

Which is what I did, approaching the then deliverance minister for Hereford to ask him what kind of a job he thought this would be for a woman.

'A very dangerous one,' he said.

3   Midwinter

Under the window, a fourteenth-century bishop slept on, his marble
mitre like a nightcap. But the tomb of his saintly predecessor, Thomas
Cantilupe, was in pieces — stone sections laid out, Merrily thought,
like a display of postmodern garden ornaments.

Midwinter of the Spirit

Midwinter enters the old city of Hereford, its cathedral, its secret history.

The deliverance consultant is appointed by the Bishop, who must approve any major exorcism. To put
Merrily right at the heart of things, I gave her an office at the cathedral and a time-share in the Bishop's lay-secretary, Sophie Hill, a smart, elegant, slightly severe woman who 'works for the Cathedral'.

Sophie's office, and Merrily's Hereford deliverance base, is above the gatehouse, overlooking Broad Street and the Cathedral green. Across the road in Gwynne Street, is the home of the former diocesan exorcist, Canon Thomas Dobbs, a man bitterly opposed to the idea of a woman deliverance consultant, pointing out that 'the first exorcist was Jesus Christ'. Dobbs is determined that Merrily should be exposed to deliverance at its most disturbing.

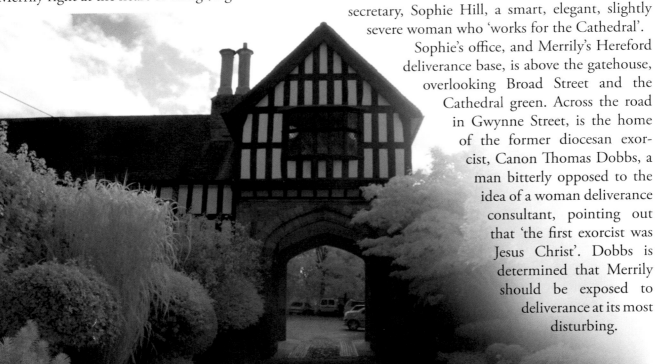

As *Midwinter* opens, she's learning about the rules and techniques of exorcism in a remote part of the Brecon Beacons, where the SAS do their training (and where exorcism *is* taught). The course leader and Merrily's spiritual director is the Rev. Huw Owen, blunt, cynical but far from sceptical. The danger of being a woman exorcist? Huw doesn't dress it up.

... headlights floated down the valley, a long way away. She thought of Jane back home in Ledwardine and felt isolated, cut off. A night breeze razored down from crags she could no longer see.

'Listen,' Huw said, 'the ordination of women is indisputably the most titillating development in the Church since the Reformation. They'll follow you home, they'll breathe into your phone at night, break into your vestry and tamper with your gear. Crouch in the back pews and masturbate through your sermons ... prime target for every psychotic grinder of the dark satanic mills that ever sacrificed a chicken ...'

Merrily's first assignment takes her to the old Hereford General Hospital, once the city's lunatic asylum, where she encounters a patient who makes even seasoned nurses nervous. This incident is based almost entirely on a story I was told by a local former nursing sister.

Fairly soon, a body is recovered from the River Wye near Victoria Bridge, not far from the old hospital and the story switches to Dinedor Hill and the Cathedral and the ancient church of St Cosmas and St Damien, by way of the Dinedor ley and the legacy of

You won't find an official monument to Alfred Watkins in Hereford — an almost criminal omission. There used to be a short footpath by the side of Tesco called Watkins Way, but even that disappeared. All that remains is the plaque on his former house near the Cathedral.

Watkins was a county councillor, a magistrate, a brewer, a pioneer photographer, an archaeologist and, for thousands of people all over the world, the most important Herefordian in history. For this was the man who discovered leys.

OK, *I* don't know whether or not leys exist. All I know is that the *idea* of them changed the way I look at a landscape, gave me a feel for patterns of hills and meadows, mounds and churches that I never had before. Or maybe, subliminally, I did. Maybe we all do; whatever, Alfred Watkins's contribution to our perception of Britain is unique.

A ley is a — usually invisible — line which Watkins believed linked ancient monuments. He worked out that many Bronze Age ritual sites — standing stones, stone circles, burial mounds — had been arranged to follow straight lines across the countryside. As many medieval and pre-medieval churches were built on sites of earlier worship and castle mottes were sometimes formed around burial mounds, they would also sometimes occur on straight lines. Watkins presented his theories to the Woolhope Naturalists' Field Club which, of course, still exists, and published them in *Early British Trackways* and his most celebrated work, *The Old Straight Track*, a book which continues to change lives.

Alfred Watkins' orginal research was conducted on maps and on foot. If you stand on the edge of the Iron Age camp on Dinedor Hill and look across the city you can actually see one of his most famous leys. Stand where you can align the Cathedral tower with the spire of All Saints and you're on it.

What does this mean?

Watkins was a little cagey about it. He rarely went further than the suggestion that leys were ancient trackways, possible trading routes. But when you read between the lines of *The Old Straight Track* it's clear that he was sensing a greater mystery.

It was left to a succession of later writers to develop the more seductive theories. The occultist Dion Fortune was the first to suggest, in her novel *The Goatfoot God*, that Watkins' leys might be channels of psychic energy, a theory adopted by dowsers, who began to track the lines with rods and pendulums, and developed by John Michell in his seminal book, *The View over Atlantis*.

Sketch map of the ley line running between Dinedor Camp and the church of Saints Cosmas and Damien

The latest theory, promoted by the writer Paul Devereux and others, is that leys were 'spirit roads', routes along which the dead were believed to walk and where tribal shamans sought communication with them. Supporting evidence for this includes the tradition of 'coffin paths' — established routes by which the dead were taken into country churches, seen as memories of leys — and, of course, the tendency for ghost sightings to be reported on leys.

The narrow Church Street, or Capuchin Way, which links Hereford Cathedral with High Town follows one of Watkins' leys. This is where Merrily's friend, Lol Robinson lives in *Midwinter of the Spirit*.

But the Dinedor ley, passing through the centre of the city and the cathedral itself, is central to the plot ... and one of the few it's possible to see almost from beginning to end.

Dinedor Hill

... is often said to be Hereford's mother hill. This may be where the city began, as an Iron Age camp, the ramparts of which can still be seen in the shade of mature trees at the top of the hill.

Although the name Dinedor comes from the ancient British or Welsh *dyn*, meaning fort, the earthworks on the hill suggest a community rather than a military base, and the idea of an earlier ritual site on the hill has been strengthened by the recent discovery of the Dinedor Serpent or Rotherwas Ribbon, of which more later.

If we follow the line to Hereford Cathedral we encounter the shrine of

This shrine was probably second only to Thomas Becket's in Canterbury Cathedral as a centre of healing. Candles may still be lit at the refurbished tomb in the north transept.

Born around 1218, Tommy Canty, as he's affectionately known to Merrily's spiritual director, Huw Owen, was the most celebrated medieval bishop of Hereford, a man revered in his lifetime who, it was said, could bring little birds to the window when he celebrated mass. An experienced lawyer, he was appointed Bishop of Hereford in 1275, in the reign of Edward I. In a dispute with the Archbishop of Canterbury, Thomas was excommunicated, went to Rome to appeal to the Pope and died of a fever. His body was boiled to remove the flesh and his bones brought back to Hereford, where they were entombed, originally in the Lady Chapel before a new shrine was built in the north transept in 1287.

By this time, miracles were being reported, beginning with the calming of a Hereford ironmonger's wife who, possibly because of a drink problem, attacked her husband, bit her mother and harangued God and the neighbours. She claimed to have a vision of 'Saint' Thomas, although he wouldn't be canonised until 1320.

About 500 miraculous cures were claimed over the next twenty-five years, with pilgrims being carried into the cathedral on stretchers and walking out. People too ill to be carried to the Cathedral were measured in string which was then used as the wick of a candle dedicated to St Thomas. Animals, too, were cured.

Around the time *Midwinter* was taking shape, the tomb was dismantled for cleaning, repair and refurbishment, for the first time since 1860 when, I was told, something very disturbing was found inside. Not this time, however.

As far as I know.

All Saints Church, Hereford

...is the next point on the ley.

With its flourishing café, All Saints on a weekday has a real feel of what you imagine a church would have been like in medieval times, the vibrant centre of a community. It also has a ghost who likes to sit near the organ. And, talking of organs, in the café area upstairs there's a carving which suggests a male sheelagh-na-gig ... a rampant little figure linked to fertility.

The healing theme of the Dinedor ley is picked up again at its final point.

The Church of St Cosmas and St Damien

This mysterious little double-naved church in the hamlet of Stretford, near Dilwyn, is dedicated to two 4th-century saints linked with physicians and surgeons and, although made redundant in 1969, was used until quite recently for an annual thanksgiving service for doctors and nurses.

A healing well is said to have disappeared from the church precincts, although many people still regard it as a centre of healing, and ley-hunters have pointed to some old stones in the raised church-yard as evidence of pagan worship. However, when we visited the church in March 2007 for a TV programme which, in the end, was never made, archaeologist Jodie Lewis suggested the stones might actually be the remains of the holy well.

St Cosmas and St Damien has been maintained by the Churches Conservation Trust,

remains consecrated, and occasional services are still held there ...

... unlike some churches along the Border which have fallen into disuse and, in a few cases, into ruins. Reverting, some would say, to their ancient origins as circles of stone ...

4 Witchlights

> Curtains of cold, red light hung from the heavens into the roofless nave. When Robin emerged from the tower, she took his cold hand in her even colder ones. The church was mournful around her.
>
> *A Crown of Lights*

Now it's coming up to Candlemas, or Imbolc, the old Celtic festival of the first light, celebrated in early February, and we slip into mid-Wales, directly into the path of ...

The Dragon

There are five medieval churches in and around Radnor Forest, all dedicated to St Michael, the archangel responsible for dealing with dragons.

We lived in Radnor for over fifteen years, and although I never actually saw a dragon I did once photograph what ghost-hunters like to call 'an orb' and ufologists like to call, um, a UFO, over Castell Crugeryr, a very prominent castle mound off an elbow of road near Forest Inn.

Castell Crugeryr in snow

Tomen Castle on the lower slopes of Radnor Forest

The Four Stones

Discoed

It's an odd place, Radnor Forest. Not a forest in the accepted sense, as it actually has comparatively few trees. Forest, traditionally, was just a term for a hunting ground. This is an area of wild green hills, and the smallest hills are the castle mounds, several — Castell Crugeryr, Tomen Castle, New Radnor Castle, Hundred House Mount — visible from the country lanes known as the A44 and A481 which slither across it.

The Forest also has some nicely-obscure prehistoric stones — notably the Four Stones near Kinnerton, which appear in the third Merrily novel, *A Crown of Lights*.

Behind a hedge, this is a safe, almost cosy site from which to contemplate the quarry-savaged skyline and the lofty Old Radnor church to the west.

Old Radnor, dominant though it appears, is not one of the five St Michael churches which form a slightly squashed pentagram across the hills, extending from Cefnllys — lovely spot — near Llandrindod Wells, up to Llanfihangel Rhydithon, down to Llanfihangel-nant-Melan, Cascob and finally Discoed with its venerable yew tree, close to the English border.

A stretch of hillside near Llandegley, in the Forest, is still known as The Dragon's Back, and a former clergyman at Llanfihangel Rhydithon wrote,

> I often spoke to an old man who lived up on the slopes of the Forest and maintained that though he had never seen it he had heard it breathing. Was it because of the dragon that our Christian ancestors ringed it around with St Michael churches ...?

Several sources suggest that Radnor Forest was particularly vulnerable to the forces of darkness and required protection at the highest level. One legend warns that if any of the churches is allowed to close, the evil will return.

But what was meant by evil?

Is the dragon simply a symbol of the ancient pagan religions represented by the standing stones, circles and mounds all over Radnor Forest? (As *A Crown of Lights* was being written, archaeologists were documenting the discovery of a massive henge in the Radnor Valley, not far from the location of the novel's one invented village, Old Hindwell.) Or was there believed to be a real and active evil which could be repelled only be a combination of old and new religion?

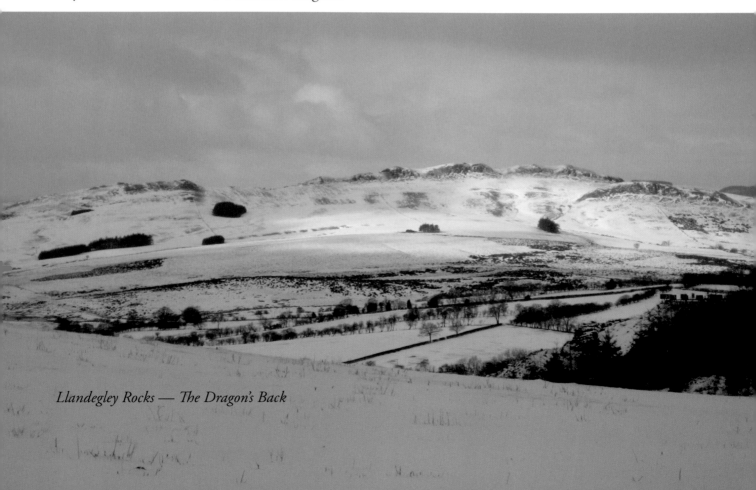

Llandegley Rocks — The Dragon's Back

The idea for *A Crown of Lights* began to ferment when a member of an old Radnorshire family, Glyn Morgan, sent me a copy of a charm found in a farmhouse in north Radnorshire invoking holy names to protect the farmer, his horses, cows, sheep, pigs and poultry from molestation, witches' spells and the power of Satan.

Its mixture of Christianity and paganism was remarkably similar to a well-known exorcism which you can still see on a wall of the most remote of St Michael churches at Cascob. Dating back to round 1700, it's known as the Abracadabra Charm because of its traditional use of a magic word since devalued by generations of stage magicians.

A B R A C A D A B R A
A B R A C A D A B
A B R A C A D
A B R A C
A B R
A

In the name of the Father, son and the Holy Ghost Amen x x x and in the name of the Lord Jesus Christ I will deliver Elizabeth Loyd from all witchcraft and from all Evil spirites & from all evil men or Women or Wizardes or hardness of hart Amen x x x

The site of Ednol Church; (above) the ruins of Llanwarne (opposite)

So was there, in Radnor Forest, a hybrid religion, a form of semi-pagan hedge-Christianity, and what remains of it today?

In *A Crown of Lights*, a pagan couple move into a farmhouse and are presented by 'the local people' with a copy of a similar protective charm, before becoming the target of what is effectively a witch hunt led by a fundamentalist Anglican priest with a few secrets of his own.

The farmhouse happens to have, on its land, a ruined church, which forms part of the protective pentagram of St Michael churches. To avoid ruining the reputation of an existing ruined church, I had to invent one. However there is one in Radnor Forest, Ednol, of which rather less remains than the church at Old Hindwell. There are also a couple of ruins in Herefordshire which fit the image. The first is at Llanwarne, a few miles from Ross-on-Wye. And the other — which also serves as an introduction to the Frome Valley, location of the next chapter — illustrates another aspect of exorcism.

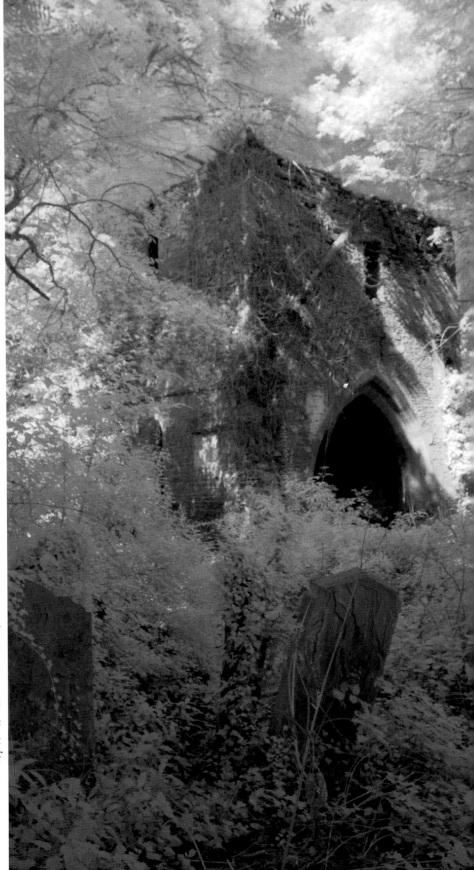

Avenbury Church

The remains of St Mary's, Avenbury, lie in a shallow grave of tangled woodland, enclosed by tall trees, embalmed by creepers. Mentioned in the Domesday Book of 1086, the church was decommissioned by the diocese in 1946 ... and if you're alone here at dusk, just be grateful for the silence.

The ghost stories have been circulating for at least fifty years. It's said that a church organ sometimes moans at close of day. That bells peel in the roofless tower. That a company of cowled monks still sings in the opened shell of the nave.

'No, I don't particularly like the place,' the Rev. Graham Sykes says carefully. 'It makes me feel uneasy.'

Graham, vicar of Bromyard in East Herefordshire, is responsible for the former parish of Avenbury where this church was left to rot. It might be a thousand years old, but it was never an architectural treasure. Another local vicar has visited it just once and has no plans to return.

'It's a horrible place. It just *feels* horrible. I've never been anywhere before where I've felt so much ... badness.'

But it's not the ghostly monks that offend the local clergy, or the spooky soundtrack. It's the fact that St Mary's still seems to be a place of worship.

The wrong kind, of course. Like many medieval churches, it's believed to occupy a place of pre-Christian sanctity, and its absentee owner actually erected a sign identifying it as an 'ancient pagan site'. So now, as its stonework crumbles, St Mary's has become fully available, day and night, for ... well, for anything you fancy, basically.

Amongst the rubble below the tower's last remaining rafter, I found signs of a recent fire and the remains of candles burned on the broken graves of local families. The suspicion, naturally, is of black magic rites or at least occult games involving teenagers attracted by the church's sinister reputation and its isolation.

'I do think places are affected by the things that happen in them,' Graham Sykes says. 'I think kids have been going out there, maybe at night, for a laugh.'

But when the laughter dies and they go home alone, perhaps wondering what they might have disturbed ... that's often when the problems begin.

As recently as last year, a small outbreak of apparent poltergeist phenomena was reported at homes in the area — moving objects, footsteps heard overhead, cold spots. Several of these cases were said to have involved families known to be fascinated by the ruins of St Mary's Church. The talk was of ouija-board experiments — attempts to contact the unquiet dead of Avenbury.

As the building isn't theirs any more, there's nothing the Church can do about whatever goes on there. Besides, paganism is an accepted faith and these days even satanists are likely to claim their religious rights. Christian clergy can only address what they perceive to be the spiritual or psychological effects of what may or may not be happening.

"I think,' Graham Sykes says, 'that if people dabble with the occult then it affects them — disturbs their psyche. And it can manifest in psycho-kinetic energy. I think they're playing with fire.'

Graham remains unconvinced by the old ghost-stories at Avenbury, suggesting its bad atmosphere may have more to do with what's been happening there *since* it became known as a haunted ruin.

'I think that it's been spiritually damaged by people playing around ... and *that's* why it's an uneasy place. Some places do need to be healed. But first, the *people* need to be healed.'

Which brings us to *The Cure of Souls*.

5   Lady of the Bines

A second black pole appeared, rearing hard against the
northern sky, and this one had a short crosspiece like —
his first thought — a gibbet. From it hung something limp
and shrivelled, the skeletal spine of a dead garland;
when he passed between the two poles his bare elbow
brushed against the remains with a dry, papery crackle.
Now he could see the extent of it: dozens of black poles
against the pale night, in lines to either side of him across
the barren ground ... like a site laid out for a mass-crucifixion.

The Cure of Souls

So where do you get your ideas?

As this is acknowledged worldwide as the most blindingly
obvious question aimed at novelists, you'd think people would be
embarrassed to ask it by now. But they aren't, and I actually have
an answer, apart from the one that goes, 'I buy them at night off
this guy in dark glasses and a hoodie on the edge of the Plascarreg
Estate.'

The simple answer is: they come out of the location. You find a
place that looks interesting, examine its history, ancient and recent,
and its folklore, look at its current preoccupations, stir them all
together and add a crime. That's it, really.

The Cure of Souls is set in the Frome Valley of eastern
Herefordshire. Not the most widely known area of the county.
Places quite near to an established tourist area seldom are, and the
Frome Valley will always be in the shadow of the Malverns. Its hills
are discreet and its river is usually unobtrusive. As Lol Robinson
sings,

Looking across the Frome Valley to the Malverns, and one its hop fields and old kilns (opposite)

> The River Frome goes nowhere in particular
> It isn't very wide
> There's nothing on the other side.

Actually, Lol may have been using the Frome Valley as a metaphor for the condition of his life at the time. As the novel opens, he's working in the (fictional) village of Knight's Frome — not far from Bishop's Frome and Canon Frome — as assistant to Prof Levin, the music producer, now assembling his own recording studio there.

Nearby is a converted hop kiln. Not unusual in the Frome Valley, where very few hop kilns these days are used for the hops which were once, thanks to its lush, deep soil, the valley's biggest industry.

Hops

... put the flavour in beer. They are related to nettles and cannabis. The hop plant climbs clockwise around its pole and can reach twenty feet, dying back to the soil every winter. After picking — a major operation — they are dried in hop kilns, which pierce the skyline across the Frome and Lugg Valleys.

38

It was an intoxicatingly mysterious world, full of arcane terms like hop-crib and hop-devil, and the smell of sulphur. But now, thanks to cheap hops from Off, the Herefordshire industry is in serious decline. Many hopyards have fallen into dereliction. And a derelict hopyard is a spooky place, as Lol discovers in *The Cure of Souls*.

Before cheap hops from Off, the biggest scourge was the voracious Verticillium Wilt, which would put acres of hopyard into quarantine, symbolised in the novel by The Lady of the Bines, a spectral figure haunting hopyards. If you see her, your crop is doomed.

Just as strawberries in the polytunnels further west are now picked mainly by East Europeans, the hops used to be picked by incoming seasonal labour, the Valleys people from South Wales, the Dudleys from the Black Country and — most interesting, as far as this novel is concerned, the gypsies — mainly ...

Romanies

'Romanies respect, sometimes consult the ancestors, but they let the dead lie. Don't ever trust the dead. We have a word ... *mulo* ... the Romani word for a ghost. This word is also used for a vampire. The living dead.

   We don't worry about your dead — we'll settle down to sleep in your cemeteries any night of the week. We believe that the Romani dead ... they don't come back for no reason. We're very afraid of the vengeful power of our dead.'

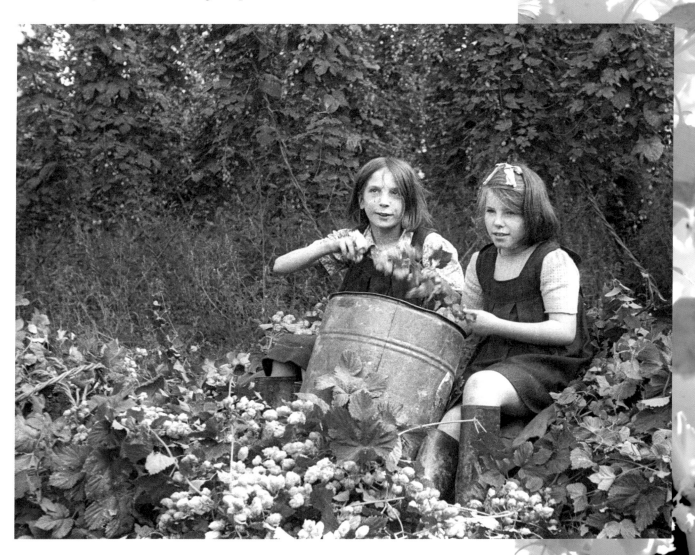

This is Al Boswell talking. In the novel Al is the Romani craftsman behind the famous Boswell Guitar, known these days, thanks to modern marketing, as *The Lute of the Frome*. This much-prized instrument is fashioned from a carefully chosen mixture of woods, which are taken sparingly without the destruction of a single tree. The philosophy of 'borrowing the earth' was borrowed from Patrick Jasper Lee's book, which explains the methods of the *Chovihano*, or Romani shaman. I learned a lot from this book and others possibly out of print now.

For example ... a Romani ghost may appear not at dead of night, but dead of noon. In the brightest sunlight, *the time of no shadows*. A nice twist.

I promise there are no vampires in this, or any of the books. But *The Cure of Souls* does deal with some of the central problems of deliverance: when to exorcise and how far to go, with the atmosphere of a converted hop kiln apparently disturbed as a result of a murder committed there.

Just occasionally a novel happens the other way round, starting not with location but with murder. If it's real murder you're on dangerous ground.

The font at Castle Frome Church

6 A Dark Lamp

Fred's leaning across, apologising to Rose. 'Now I know you
won't mind, my love, but we gotter drop Jane off in Ledwardine ...'
The Lamp of the Wicked

In this scene, Merrily is dreaming, and it's not the kind of dream anyone needs. But the nightmare grin of the goblinesque mass-murderer Fred West seems destined to become an image out of folklore, swimming up from the darkest undercurrent in rural Herefordshire.

The scale of Fred's evil may never be fully known, the investigation having ended — arguably because of the cost — rather prematurely in my view. But then, what do I know?

More than I feel comfortable with, to be honest. When I first thought of the theme of *The Lamp of the Wicked*, my wife urged me to leave it alone. It was all too recent, the pain too close to the surface.

Fred West was found hanged in his cell before he could stand trial for the murders of women and girls at the home he shared with his wife Rosemary in Cromwell Street, Gloucester. Rose is now serving life for her part in the murders. Fred was a builder and knew how to dispose of bodies under concrete. As a result there were lots of black jokes about patios — the British way of dealing with it.

But, in the end, it was never really dealt with to anyone's satisfaction and its aftermath still hangs like noxious industrial smoke over Gloucester, Herefordshire and the Forest of Dean.

And I kept running into people connected with the case or the West family.

A neighbour of ours recalled some amusing but, with hindsight, slightly sinister stories about a relative of Fred who, apparently, had once worked ... well, very close to where we live. Geoffrey Wansell, who wrote (very much against the clock, so that it could hit the shelves in the wake of Rose's trial) the first and most explicit West biography, *An Evil Love*, would tell me how, after listening to the tapes of Fred's interrogation by police, he would go into the church near his home to try and remove the aura of raw evil they always left behind. Gordon Burn, author of the devastating *Happy like Murderers*, told me he never wanted to deal with a subject this dark again, ever.

But Prof. Bernard Knight, the pathologist who conducted autopsies on several of the victims, pointed out that aspects of the case were still ... unresolved. The implications were extremely sinister, and I decided to go ahead.

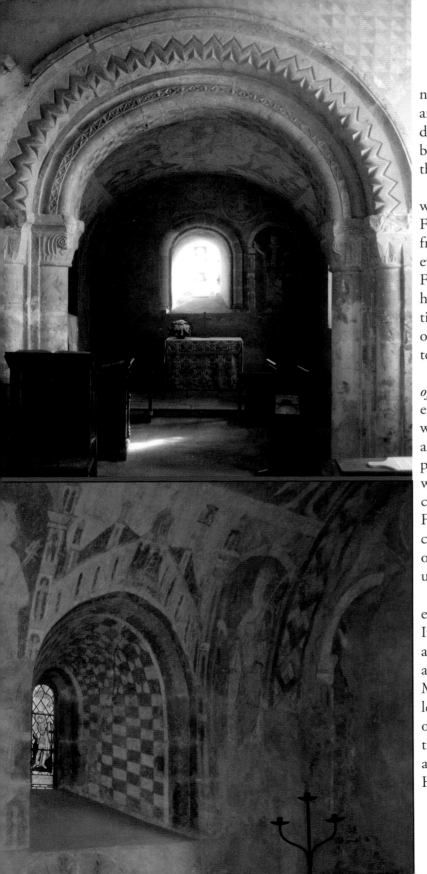

Fiction can often say more than speculative non-fiction, but this is the darkest in the series and some readers prefer to avoid it. Personally, I don't think that what the Wests did should ever be forgotten, if only because there's a lot more that needs to come out.

Fred West was born in Much Marcle where, after his arrest, bodies were discovered in Fingerpost field — a lovely spot, actually, not far from the idyllic Kempley Church with its medieval murals. Because he ended up in Gloucester, Fred is usually seen as a low-life city boy; in fact, he was very much a Welsh Border man: practical, independent, self-sufficient. He killed out of expediency and always (to use building trade terminology) 'made good' afterwards.

However, I was determined that *The Lamp of the Wicked* should deal less with the sickening reality of life in Cromwell Street than with the emotional aftermath over a very wide area of western Britain. There are dozens of parents, siblings and boyfriends of missing girls who, not least because the case was too rapidly closed, will never know if they were victims of Fred and Rose. Most people connected with the case believe that many more victims — forty is one informed estimate — may be lying in their unmarked graves.

Lamp is about a man apparently influenced, several years later, by the West murders. It's not, I hope, a gruesome or a sadistic novel as much as an emotional one. But it is dark, and it would have been unfair to burden Much Marcle with a fictional development of the West legend, so I switched the scene to nearby Ross-on-Wye, and the Coughton Valley. Because of the nature of the plot it was necessary to create a new village, Underhowle, named after nearby Howle Hill. However, this is still very much a

real area, just a few miles from Symonds Yat, which was already linked with a murder by a man known as Black Dai, a Fred West copycat killer from South Wales.

Lamp also deals with the health-damaging, mind-altering effects of living under high-voltage power lines. Massive pylons carrying power to Gloucestershire stalk the Coughton Valley, and I was interested in a theory that linked electricity to so-called alien abduction. In the novel, an environmental activist sees an invisible invasion.

'If we could see all the TV and satellite signals, all the radio waves serving mobile phones, police communications, cab fleets, air networks, the sky would be this kind of poisonous black the whole day long. If we could smell them like exhaust fumes we'd all choke to death. But it's a whole lot more subtle than that. They zip unseen and unfelt through our atmosphere and our bodies and our brains ... the insidious wind that blows through us all ... flesh and tissue and bones ...'

The novel also recalls the plague that settled in Ross in 1637, with major loss of life and the town in quarantine, details of which can be found in *The Story of Ross* by Pat Hughes and Heather Hurley. They note a report by Thomas Jenkins which recalls that:

> The dead were buried at night in their wearing apparel in deep graves or pits, numbers at a time ... The bodies were brought in carts and slipped out of the carts into the grave. Good old Vicar Price used to stand on the cross solemnising the funerals by torchlight.

Ross-on-Wye. Above: The Plague Cross and St Mary's Church
Opposite, clockwise from top left: the old lock-up; gazebo tower, the Man of Ross and leaping salmon scupture;
Wye Street, leading down to the Rope Walk

Later, the minister, Philip Price, led the townsfolk through the streets at 5 am 'chanting a litany with supplications for deliverance', after which the plague is said to have abated.

This is echoed in *The Lamp of the Wicked*, in which the disposal of bodies by night is a recurrent issue. On a less-infected level, the novel also looks at evidence of the Roman town of

Ariconium

which, as local historian Brian Cave wrote, 'remains as a ghost. Though gone in body, its spirit still marks itself upon the landscape.'

Cave thought Ariconium, around what is now Weston under Penyard, near Ross, may have been built to house Roman garrisons protecting iron mines in the nearby Forest of Dean.

You can find it along the old Roman road to Gloucester. Just follow the pylons.

7 A Real Creeper

'Mr Holmes, they were the footprints of a gigantic hound.'

But where were they actually planted? On Dartmoor ... or the Welsh Border?

It's over fifty years since Maurice Campbell, chairman at the time of the Sherlock Holmes Society, published a controversial pamphlet, *The Hound of the Baskervilles: Dartmoor or Herefordshire?*

Today, the Sherlock Holmes Society is no doubt: it's Dartmoor. But the Arthur Conan Doyle Society tends to disagree. The evidence for the spectral Hound having a paw either side of the Border, between Kington and Clyro, is considerable and was explored in the sixth Merrily Watkins book, *The Prayer of the Night Shepherd*. In this novel, a hard-up hotelier, like many before him, is attempting to build a future around the most famous of all Sherlock Holmes stories.

The unnamed Night Shepherd makes a brief appearance in the Baskerville Manuscript shown to Holmes before he comes to the aid of Sir Henry Baskerville, a man who seems to have inherited a curse. In the Manuscript, it's the Night Shepherd who directs friends of the unpleasant Sir Hugo Baskerville to the spot where he's having his throat torn out.

But who directed Sir Arthur Conan Doyle to the Hound?

'I have the idea of a real creeper for the *Strand*,' Conan Doyle wrote in 1901 to Greenough Smith, editor of the London magazine that would print Sherlock Holmes stories ahead of their publication in book form.

There was one stipulation, however, Doyle said. 'I must do it with my friend Fletcher Robinson.'

Robinson, much younger, at 28, than Doyle, and from Devon, had entertained the great man, during a golfing holiday in Norfolk, with the legend of a spectral hound. Doyle was inspired.

So which legend *was* this? As far as the Holmes Society was concerned, it had to be the story of Sir Richard Cabell, the most hated man on Dartmoor, and his revenant canine companion. When Doyle and Robinson went to Devon to research the novel, the coachman who drove them around was one Harry Baskerville.

Case closed? Apparently not. The most recent Conan Doyle biography, *Teller of Tales* by Daniel Stashower, points out that Greenough Smith later recalled Robinson saying he'd found the legend in 'a Welsh guide book'. And the proposed title of the book was disclosed by Conan Doyle in a letter to his mother in Scotland before he and Robinson had been to Dartmoor or, presumably, met Harry Baskerville.

However, Welsh and Herefordshire guidebooks, to this day, often re-tell the story of ...

Hergest Court should not be confused with Hergest Croft, where the gardens are open to the public. Hergest Court, a much bleaker-looking place in a more exposed location, doesn't do gardens.

I first went there in the late 1980s to record a programme for BBC Radio Wales. The tenant farmer at the time, John Williams, remembered the 'prickly feeling' that went up his back when he once heard, from the hall, what sounded like the patter of huge paws in an upstairs room. Later, he said, he saw a hound-like shadow passing in from of him towards the inner hall.

You'll still find people in Kington who won't go down the lane to Hergest after dark. Bob Jenkins, journalist, historian and Kington oracle, told me about a man cycling to work at Kington Camp during World War Two.

'Near Hergest Court, he saw this enormous hound which he'd never seen before and never saw again. The hound had huge eyes — that's what impressed him. He had a feeling that there was something that just wasn't real about it.'

To this day, you can hear accounts of psychic disturbance at Hergest Court, and it all seems to be down to Black Vaughan — Thomas Vaughan, who lived at the Court when it was much bigger and more fortified than the present sawn-off farmhouse.

The events in the Baskerville Manuscript take place during The Great Rebellion, the English Civil War. Black Vaughan — so called, apparently, merely because of the colour of his hair — took part in the previous civil conflict, the Wars of the Roses. Vaughan changed sides, from Lancaster to York (changing sides comes easily to border people; it's about survival) and was said to have been killed at a battle near Banbury. His headless body was brought back to Kington, to be buried next to his wife Ellen Gethin ('the terrible'), who has her own legend. They now lie side by side in a rather spooky tomb in the Vaughan Chapel in Kington Parish Church.

Vaughan has been described as a notorious tyrant, although there's nothing in history to support this. It was only after death that he began to measure up to Hugo Baskerville's level of infamy, when a spectral hound was also seen, its appearances heralding death in the Vaughan family. The ghost of Vaughan himself began to exhibit signs of revenant-rage, rampaging through Kington, turning over farmers' carts and disrupting church services by manifesting as a bull. Fairly soon, nobody wanted to come to Kington Market and the town's economy began to suffer.

It was decided, at this stage, that Vaughan needed to be properly exorcised.

This was a big job that took twelve priests. Ella Mary Leather's *The Folklore of Herefordshire* tells how Vaughan appeared during the ritual, insisting he had now become a devil. Eventually subdued, after a lot of shouting and extinguishing of candles, his spirit was shrunk, confined to a snuff box — local historian Alan Lloyd suggests this was actually a candle-snuffer box — and buried under a stone at the bottom of the pool in front of Hergest Court.

Only the Hound remained, as a harbinger of death in the Vaughan family and a spectral watchdog around Hergest, where no Vaughan has resided since the death of the Rev. Silvanus Vaughan in 1706.

The final problem

So is it Dartmoor or the Welsh Border?

I think Conan Doyle's hound is a mongrel. This is what novelists do — pinch material from different sources, muddying its origins. But, as far as the hound's pedigree goes, the balance of probability falls towards the Border.

The original Baskervilles were Norman barons who came over after the conquest, building castles at Eardisley in Herefordshre and Aberedw across the border in Radnorshire. Their descendants owned the mansion Clyro Court, now the Baskerville Hall Hotel. The pub in the village of Clyro has always been The Baskerville Arms. If you look at the family tree of the Vaughans of Hergest you'll find evidence of intermarriage with the Baskervilles of Clyro.

After publication of *The Prayer of the Night Shepherd* raked up the embers of the old argument and a story in the Daily Telegraph had Hound fans snapping at each other in the paper's letters column, I had an email from Christopher Roden, of the Arthur Conan Doyle Society, who explained,

> Conan Doyle's first wife, Louise, whom he married in 1885, was one of the Hawkins of Minsterworth family. When he married her, and until her death, Louise was receiving an annuity from her brother Joseph's farms, the Bettws and Whitehall farms at Clyro. A neighbouring owner was Thomas Baskerville Mynors Baskerville, and the Hawkins farms were eventually sold to Ralph Hopton Baskerville in 1907, following Louise's death in 1906.

It's inconceivable, given such a close connection, that Conan Doyle wouldn't have visited the area at some stage.

It seems to be quite impossible that ACD would not have known the legend of Black Vaughan's demon dog.

Vaughans also married Hawkinses.

Around the same time, the late Geoffrey Hopton, last of the Hopton/Baskervilles in Clyro, told me that his grandmother's understanding of the situation had been that Conan Doyle did indeed know about

Black Vaughan and had asked if he could use the name Baskerville in his novel, as it had more resonance. The Baskervilles said yes ... as long as he located the novel somewhere else.

This was confirmed in *Out of the Shadows: The Untold Story of Conan Doyle's first family*, by a descendant, Georgina Doyle.

The final evidence, for me, is the coincidence of names. Apart from Baskerville itself, there's Mortimer — it's Dr Mortimer who first brings the problem to the attention of Sherlock Holmes. The Mortimers, of course, were for many years the most powerful Norman family in the Welsh Marches.

There's also Stapleton, the naturalist, a key character in the novel and the name of a hamlet just beyond Presteigne, a few miles from Kington.

So where's Baskerville Hall?

Although there's evidence in the cellars of an earlier building on the site, Clyro Court, former home of the Baskervilles, now the Baskerville Hall Hotel is Victorian and therefore unlikely to be Conan Doyle's model. It could be that Baskerville Hall is on Dartmoor, but if you're looking for a Welsh Border house which fits the image, it's worth investigating

Kinnersley Castle

This Welsh border stronghold, a few miles from Clyro on the Herefordshire side, was held for generations by the de la Bere family, two generations of whom are entombed in the Church of St Cosmas and St Damian at Stretford.

But in the mid 16th century it became the property of Roger Vaughan, MP for Radnorshire, and grandson of Black Vaughan himself, who spent a fortune turning a Norman castle into a state-of-the-art Tudor mansion, with tall leaded windows and a four-storey central tower.

If you want to feel the power of the Vaughans, this is the place. Over a fireplace is the emblem of the

Vaughans, a child with a snake wound around his neck. (It's been speculated that this is what gave Conan Doyle the idea for *The Speckled Band*, the one where ... well, I won't spoil it if you haven't read it) And there's a ceiling with the heads of hounds, dragons and a green man.

There are yew trees outside, close to the castle. There may have been, as at Baskerville Hall, a yew alley ...

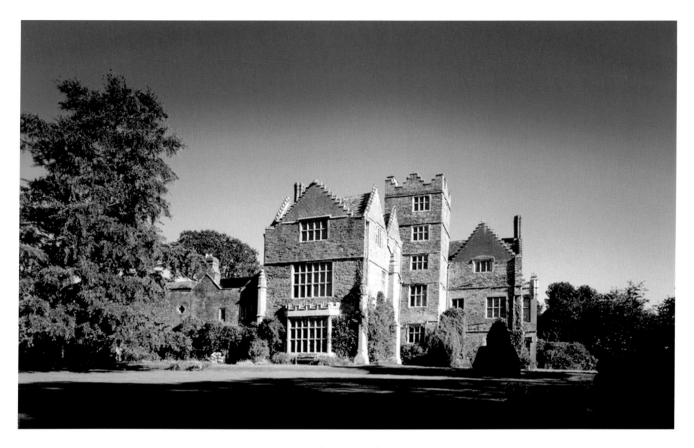

It doesn't end ...

In 1987, Jenny Vaughan, a businesswoman from the Midlands, came to Kington with a friend to investigate her family history. She didn't, fortunately perhaps, see the hound. But she did see a bull in the church where, you'll remember, the angry spirit of black Vaughan, was said to take taurine form. I talked to Jenny, for radio, inside the church, some months later.

It made very convincing radio.

> The inside of his nostrils — this was one of the most vivid things — were very, very red, like a racehorse when it's just stopped running. And it was wet. It was dripping moisture or something on to the ground. It was as though it was hanging in strings ... I'm a hard-headed business person but I can't deny it. I've seen it.

Over at Hergest Court, the hauntings, it seems, have never gone away. Tenants regularly report disturbances.

As for Hergest pool, where the spirit of Black Vaughan is supposed to lie in its snuff box, Roy Palmer records in his *Herefordshire Folklore* that when there were attempts to fill in the pool some years ago the project was abandoned after the water began to bubble ominously.

A few years ago, when the water level dropped, it was decided the pool should be cleaned out, and a large stone became visible. Historian Alan Lloyd thought this might be a good opportunity to find out if there was any kind of container underneath it and tried to persuade local farmers with mechanical diggers to check it out.

Nobody was prepared to go near. I don't even think Gomer Parry would've done it.

Stanner Rocks

Much of the action in *Prayer* takes place at the Stanner Hall Hotel, close to Stanner Rocks, said to be the oldest rocks (over 700 million years old) in Wales.

The rocks can be seen from the edge of the Kington bypass on the Welsh side, bulging out of the hillside foliage like stone age sculpture. A combination of geography and air currents means that some spots up there have an almost mediterranean climate, and Fred Slater, in *The Nature of Central Wales*, describes the rocks as a 'botanical jewel,' because of the rare — and even unique — plant species found there.

As for the Stanner Hall Hotel ... that's roughly in the vicinity of the less-decrepit Dunfield Manor, now a conference centre. Local people insist Arthur Conan-Doyle once stayed there.

It doesn't seem to be haunted.

8   A place to die for

> Merrily felt very small and exposed.
>
> She was wearing jeans and a green fleece with a torn pocket. She had a canvas shoulder bag with her cigarettes inside and her phone. Around her neck was a chain with a tiny gold cross on it that was hidden by the neck of her grey T-shirt.
>
> Disoriented in an old town like a pop-up book, coming at her from all angles in wedges of carrot-coloured antique brick and twisting timbers and thrusting gables ...
>
> *The Smile of a Ghost*

This is a novel about ... well, ghosts, kind of, but mainly about obsession. It's now slightly notorious for (a couple of years before the tragic Bridgend epidemic of 2008) having a theme of localised teenage suicide, linked, in this case, to a famous fall from the Hanging Tower of Ludlow Castle in south Shropshire.

Ludlow is a town which usually attracts less fatal obsession, but obsession nonetheless. People visit it and just *have* to live there — not only, perhaps, because of the recent boom in fancy restaurants, or even the fact that Ludlow is frequently named as the most beautiful medieval town in Britain. It could be something far more elusive, because it goes back centuries. Even three hundred years ago, the town had a reputation as a resort ... somewhere it was good just to be.

In the novel, the notoriously gothic singer, Bell Pepper, known as Belladonna, moves to Ludlow and, for reasons which, if you haven't read the novel, you wouldn't want me to explain here, begins to roam its streets and passageways at night with a candle-lamp, like a ghost.

However, the novel's, and the town's, real ghost may be someone else.

Marion de la Bruyere

There are two ways out of that tower, and I took the wrong one at first and came up against some steps that led nowhere any more, a blank wall, and that was horrifying, as if whichever way I went I'd come up

against a wall that hadn't been there when I went in. Imagination, in these situations, becomes so unbelievably powerful. So I scrambled back down and back into the chamber and ... well ... that's when I saw her.

Bernie Dunmore, Bishop of Hereford, *The Smile of a Ghost*

A lady of the castle is how Marion is usually described, which, when you think about it, could mean anything. She was probably very young when she died.

This was in the 12th century, the reign of Henry II, whose predecessor, Stephen, had given control of Ludlow Castle to a Breton knight, Joce de Dinan, who may have left his name to Dinham, the sloping community between the castle and the River Teme.

Ludlow Castle is probably the most impressive medieval stronghold along the Welsh border. It has many royal connections, and was once the military HQ for Wales. In a honeyed light, it looks deceptively mellow. Except, possibly, for the Hanging Tower.

The baronial de Lacy family, big in the area, had coveted this castle for some time, and the Lacy/Dinan conflict had led to the capture of a young knight, Arnold de Lisle. While imprisoned in the castle, Arnold formed a relationship with Marion de la Bruyere, who helped him escape down a rope or possibly knotted sheets. Unfortunately she then let him back up by rope ladder and, during their rapturous reunion, a whole bunch of heavily-armed de Lacy men shot up the ladder and took the castle. Soon afterwards, there was much slaughter and destruction in the town to make it clear that de Lacy was now in control.

When she saw what she'd done, the remorseful Marion killed Arnold with his own sword and then, fearing either repercussions from Joce or gang-rape by de Lacy's heavies, threw herself from the highest window in the Hanging Tower. It was said that her final anguished screams could be heard for years afterwards before they were reduced to a breathing sound. In *A Gazetteer of British Ghosts*, Peter Underwood recalled a Ludlow man, Mr J. Didlick, 'who told me that the sounds might be likened to those made by someone in very deep sleep'.

So maybe she's at peace now.

I couldn't find Mr Didlick, but the Hanging Tower may be viewed from inside the castle, now owned by the Earl of Powis, whose home castle at Welshpool is in far better repair.

But, for a more dramatic — and cheaper — view of the tower, follow the public footpath to the right of the castle, as you approach it from the town centre. You'll eventually arrive at the yew tree under Marion's window, the subject of the chapter entitled *Tonguing the Yew*, in *The Smile of a Ghost*.

(Health and Safety warning: don't tongue the yew. Yews are very poisonous.)

Anyway, this is a significant point on Bell Pepper's ghostwalk, which you might prefer to start from the other end of town, beginning in

Possibly my all-time favourite cemetery can be reached from the bottom of Corve Street by following the path alongside the former church, which now serves as a printing and copying workshop. The disused graveyard itself — and it's fair to say not everybody thinks this is a good thing — has been allowed to become atmospherically overgrown as a wildlife haven. It will lead you to some nicely-framed and unexpectedly green views of the castle across the town.

In fact, it's possible to walk from here to the castle avoiding all prominent streets or rarely encountering, even in high season, too many people ... although ghosts can't be ruled out as you wander through the yards of one-time coaching inns, up and down stone steps, along narrow alleyways, catching ribbons of conversation through open back doors as whole centuries seem to drop away.

You need to stop in the Linney, the steep, narrow street backing on to the castle's curtain wall before curving down to the River Teme. All very clean and refined now but it's easy to imagine medieval human detritus in full foetid flow down the earthen gutters to the river.

You will, by now, have passed through the shadow of the church sometimes called the Beacon of the Marches.

The Church of St Laurence

I once stayed in the centre of Ludlow for two months, while starting a new job, and the church clock awoke me every hour on the hour all through the night. It's been quietened now, which is a shame in a way. But the church is still as big a presence in the old town as the castle, and its foundations may be even older, built, as they were, out of a neolithic mound, presumably the *low* in Ludlow.

St Laurence's, as you can see from the amazing vantage point at Whitcliffe — don't miss this view — is the centre of the wheel of Ludlow. If you have the stamina and a head for heights, you can climb to the top of the tower, scene of the climax of *Smile*, and take in dizzying views of the castle, the town and Clee Hill beyond. The vertig-

inous should at least check out the Palmers' Window inside the church, which commemorates

The Palmers' Guild

A palmer was a medieval pilgrim to the Holy Land who brought back a palm frond as evidence of having done the trip. The Palmers' Guild was mystically linked to the cult of King Edward the Confessor and to St John. You can get an idea of all this possibly-wishful thinking in the impressive 15th century eight-paned Palmers' stained-glass window. More than just a collection of 'what we did on our pilgrimage' snaps.

The Guild, consisting mainly of wealthy businessmen, was formed to employ priests whose main function was to pray for the souls of Guild members and their families. In those days, buying a stairway to heaven was as legitimate as taking out a pension fund and, indeed, the Guild also fulfilled a similar role in supporting members who fell on hard times.

It's difficult, without one of those *look away now* moments, to explain the significance, in this novel, of the Palmers' Guild. But it's worth noting that, while there were similar guilds all over Britain, Ludlow's achieved national prominence.

9   Music of the Spheres

'Drivers reckoned they swerved to avoid a ghost,' Spicer said.

His tone hadn't altered and his eyes remained limpid. A wood pigeon's hollow call was funnelled out of the valley.

'That took a while to come, didn't it?' Merrily said.

The Remains of an Altar

Altar begins — and perhaps ends — with a ghost story, and the idea for the novel began with a real one.

A few years ago, villagers at Stoke Lacy, in eastern Herefordshire, came to believe that the road through their community was haunted, following a series of unexplained road accidents.

Most accidents involve more than one vehicle, maybe one driver swerving to avoid another. In Stoke Lacy, vehicles were leaving the road in isolation, drivers saying it felt as if someone else was moving the steering wheel. It happened so many times that an exorcism was suggested, and there was consultation with the man who was standing in, at the time, for Merrily Watkins.

However, the deliverance minister for Hereford had a problem with it. For a start, there was no back-story — no famous death-crash in the past, no suggestion of an unquiet spirit which might benefit from a Requiem Eucharist, or even an imprint or place-memory. In the end he was unconvinced and took no action.

The only solution was offered by members of the British Association of Dowsers, who surveyed the road with rods and pendulums and concluded that the problem had been caused by the siting of a millennial stone in a wood which they suggested may have been disrupting the energy flow, causing a reflex reaction in the motorists.

Either way, it made me think about unexplained road accidents, and that's how *The Remains of an Altar* begins — although not in Stoke Lacy — as Merrily Watkins is called in to investigate similar, if more extreme, accidents in the village of Wychehill.

To find the general area of this troubled community, take the main road north-east from Ledbury and turn left by the hotel near the British Camp car-park. This puts you in the Malvern Hills ... which really are the remains of an altar.

We live just below the Black Mountains, and the Malverns are our easterly horizon. It's clear to anyone who lives or walks or drives around this area that there's a link between the Black Mountains of Wales and the Malverns (from the Welsh *moel bryn* — bald hill) of England. Two great, sacred shelves of rock enclosing Herefordshire's landscaped garden of lush pastures, orchards and hopyards.

The English Heritage publication *The Malvern Hills, an Ancient Landscape*, by Mark Bowden, with David Field and Helen Winton, confirmed what I'd always felt: these hills, with the lofty earthworks of Herefordshire Beacon and Midsummer Hill, *were* the remains of an altar. Sacred. Untouchable. Full of earth energy and the lifeforce of water.

The Victorian spa of Great Malvern tapped into the healing power of mineral waters, but there was something here that was clearly recognised in Celtic and pre-Celtic times, when the earthworks were taking shape.

And later, inbetween the Celtic and Victorian eras, 'it is tempting,' say the authors of *An Ancient Landscape*, 'to consider the Malvern Hills as a "ritual landscape" in the medieval period as much as in the prehistoric periods'. The book goes on to identify the hills as a magnet for early Christian hermits, spiritually challenged by the desolation and that sense of exposure, not only to the elements but to 'ancient practices and spirits'.

Out of Celtic Christian hermitages came the spiritual strongholds of Great Malvern and Little Malvern priories: '... the priorities are not ordinary parish churches but rather the bases of religious "elite forces".'

Which somehow confirmed my idea of having an ex-SAS man as the vicar of Wychehill, letting me into some of the legends of The Regiment, based in Hereford.

But it was never going to be easy, or even possible, to write a novel set in the Malvern Hills without involving another legend — Britain's most famous composer.

I didn't know all that much about Sir Edward Elgar beyond the usual clichés: Master of the King's Music, Pomp and Circumstance, making Britain mightier yet ... This stiff, slightly aloof establishment figure wheeled out annually for The Last Night of the Proms.

However, after a few months' serious research, I was looking at a very different person: Ed, the Worcester piano-tuner's son who married above his class. Ed, the paranoid perfectionist, insecure, depressive, often in despair over his work. A man who actually loved *the country* more than The Country. Who wrote brilliant music but is too often associated with words he *didn't* write. Whose high-Catholicism was sometimes challenged by an instinctive paganism. Whose friend and confidante, for some years, seems to have been his daughter's white rabbit, Peter.

And then there was another friend ...

Ed And Alf

For some years, Edward Elgar, the composer, and Alfred Watkins, who discovered leys, were neighbours in Hereford.

This isn't widely known. But then, why would it be? While Hereford's connection with Elgar is always being underlined in the city and the pages of the *Hereford Times*, Watkins, who was born here and served Hereford all his working life, still gets more recognition outside. Far more.

It's bloody criminal, really. Sorry ... I keep going on about this. There should be an Alfred Watkins Museum and visitor centre in Hereford, but I expect the Establishment is worried about attracting undesirables with walking boots and dowsing rods.

Anyway, Elgar's famous residence, Plas Gwyn, now flats, is on the corner of the road which led to Watkins' house, The Vineyard, where he lived before moving into the centre of the city.

Ed and Alfred were born within a year of one another. Both were into photography and gadgets. Elgar had a dark-room at Plas Gwyn and would have been fascinated by Watkins' various photographic inventions, including the first light-meter.

And then there was the countryside. Both were members of the Woolhope Naturalists' Field Club. Both were drawn to a pastoral, very British kind of mysticism.

Why is this connection never referred to in major biographies of either of them?

I don't know, but it seemed like an interesting thread for the novel.

I was haunted particularly by Elgar's *Cello Concerto* which, although it was written after he'd moved away from Malvern, seems to reflect the evening light and shadows on the hills and the *movement* of the hills. It was the *Cello Concerto*, on an early gramophone record, that drifted around the room where Elgar lay dying and which he whistled to a friend before he said,

> If ever you're walking on the Malvern Hills and hear that, don't be
> frightened ... it's only me.

And it *is* him. He haunts those hills. Especially Herefordshire Beacon with the earthworks on top like a dented sandwich cake.

Elgar's choral epic, *Caractacus*, recalls the legend (long ago discredited) that this was the site of the Ancient British hero's last stand against the Romans. The music is full of numinous shapes in the woods and

76

druidic blood-ritual ... and it goes way over the top, thanks to the librettist's determination to turn it into a hymn to a British Empire far wider than Rome's puny effort.

'I did suggest we should dabble in patriotism in the Finale,' Elgar wrote later, 'when, lo!, the worder, instead of merely paddling his feet goes & gets naked & wallows in it ...'

All Elgar wallowed in was the mystery and the energy of the countryside, as he pedalled along the lanes around his home at Birchwood on his beloved bike Mr Phoebus — commemorated in the bronze sculpture on the cathedral green in Hereford — not far, as it happens, from Alfred Watkins's last home. Ed is leaning on Mr Phoebus peering up at the Cathedral, with big trees on either side, and on the plinth it says,

This is what I get every day. The trees are singing my music — or am I singing theirs?

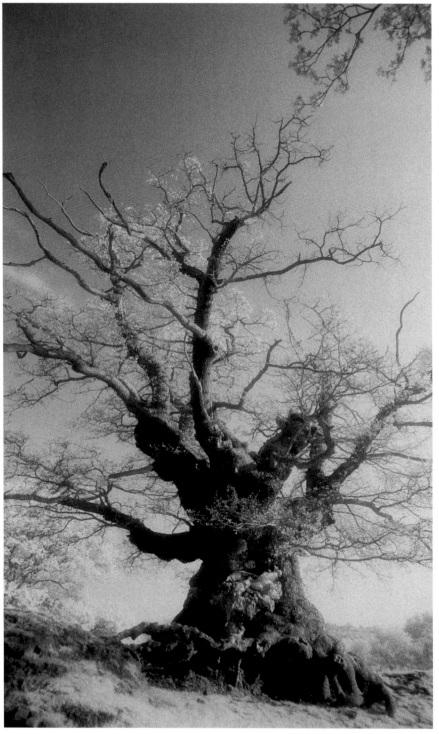

Elgar loved trees, was moved and inspired by them. While living in the south of England he once took his friend and musical collaborator Algernon Blackwood, ritual magician and author of classic ghost stories, including *The Man Whom the Trees Loved*, to see some oaks near his home which were said to be monks bewitched. He loved that story.

So it seemed inconceivable that Elgar, with that passion for trees and the interest in druidic ritual displayed in *Caractacus*, was not intimately familiar with the

Whiteleafed Oak

You'll find the oak — well, several of them — at the end of the Malvern Hills, almost exactly at the meeting point of the counties of Herefordshire, Worcestershire and Gloucestershire, the three counties that come together for the annual Three Choirs Festival, for which Elgar composed some of his finest sacred music.

This is also the centre of the circle of Perpetual Choirs, which I first read about in the works of John Michell, the writer who rediscovered Alfred Watkins in the 1960s and raised him to a new level of international fame in books including *The View over Atlantis*.

Essentially, Michell developed what Watkins himself had only

hinted at — the idea that alignments of old stones and mounds and other landscape patterns were the remains of an ancient knowledge far more advanced than history recognises ... reflecting a universal harmony most of us can no longer perceive.

The novel forms a curious link between all this and Elgar's most complex and profound choral work, *The Dream of Gerontius*, from Cardinal Newman's account of what happens to a man's soul after death ... a journey into the formal Roman Catholic afterlife with all its angelic bureaucracy. Not exactly easy-listening, often emotional and strangely tense.

And there's one moment that shoots right up your spine. A dangerous moment which the composer, conscious of sacrilege, nearly bottled, and ... this is where you need to read the novel, but it builds into an exploration of the ancient science of Pythagoras and the seductive theories of cosmic harmony and the Music of the Spheres.

And suppose Elgar *had* spent time at Whiteleafed Oak while agonising — and he really *did* agonise — over *Gerontius*?

Whiteleafed Oak is a hamlet, up a narrow lane from Hollybush, not far from Eastnor Castle. In a glass case on the village green you may find a curious little diagram related to *Harmonic Convergences* (or something). All a bit New Agey, but the significance gradually becomes apparent to Merrily Watkins in the course of *The Remains of an Altar*, as she and Lol Robinson learn about the Perpetual Choirs and meet the eccentric composer Tim Loste.

You can only reach the actual oaks on foot. It's about half a mile from the houses, across the fields. The original great oak, said to be a centre of Druid worship, at the end of a processional trail, is long gone, but its successor has been chosen. Amongst its boughs, in the wrinkles of its vast bole, you'll find offerings — ribbons and shiny things — left by recent pilgrims.

Now observe the newly-exposed views to the landmarks of the three counties.

And listen ...

10   Ghosts and Templars

> Outside, a wind had arisen, chattering amongst dead chrysanths
> in a grave pot. Merrily pulled the church keys from her shoulder
> bag. The Master House key poked out and she thrust it back ...
>
> *The Fabric of Sin*

Research for *The Fabric of Sin* uncovered the fact that not only had the Knights Templar church at Garway been visited by the — almost certainly — greatest-ever writer of ghost stories, M.R. James, but that *something happened to him there.*

Something disturbing, referred to obliquely but tantalisingly in a letter to his Herefordshire friend, Gwen MacBride.

It was a gift.

Everything in Garway seemed like a gift. Its history, its folklore, its very strange church, its dovecote with 666 dove-holes ... even the names of its pubs argued that something curious was, and may still be, at work in this landscape, a kind of inland peninsula of England dropping down to the River Monnow, on the other side of which is Wales.

It's not easy setting a novel in a very small community which actually exists. While I've always identified real towns and a few larger villages, I get cold feet about inflicting murder, feuds and iffy history on a tiny community where people and houses could easily be (wrongly) identified.

Garway, though ... with Garway, there was no way around it. And it helped that the suggestion for a Garway novel came from a very long-established and respected local family, and all the people I spoke to were well aware of what I was doing and were *still* helpful. It was necessary to create the Master House, incorporating elements of other dwellings and acting as a catalyst for the floating weirdness, but most of the rest you can visit.

But let's approach this place, initially, in the company of the writer and academic, Montague Rhodes James.

M.R. James (1862–1936)

This man is an example, still, for everybody who aspires to write a ghost story.

Although, of course, M.R. James didn't actually do ghosts. He mainly did ... things. Entities. Malevolent, terrifying entities. Think of what was inside the ash tree in the story of that name. The 'lungless laugh' from *A Warning to the Curious*. And, most important in the *Fabric of Sin* context, the 'face of crumpled linen' from *Oh Whistle and I'll Come to you, My Lad*.

A serious scholar, like several of his protagonists, Monty James, son of a clergyman in Suffolk, became provost of Eton and King's College, Cambridge, studied old manuscripts, church architecture, stained glass ... tombs.

And spent a lot of time in Herefordshire where he stayed with the widow of his friend James McBryde, who illustrated his first volume of ghost stories and died far too young. From 1906, Gwendolen McBryde and her daughter, Jane, lived near Kilpeck. Gwen seems to have been devoted to Monty in a platonic sort of way. He'd spend relaxing holidays with the McBrydes and became guardian to Jane, who displayed graphic skills from an early age and was also very fond of things emerging from gaping tombs.

Monty was especially fond of the McBrydes' second home in Herefordshire, from which he attended services at Dore Abbey. In her book, *Letters to a Friend*, Gwendolen recalled him reading the lesson in 'his fine, slightly plaintive voice ... It always gave me an unreal feeling, as if some saint held forth to lesser creatures and birds.'

Although he said Hereford Cathedral may have been one of the locations behind *The Stalls of Barchester*, the only M.R. James story set wholly in Herefordshire was *A View from a Hill*, the one involving strange visions seen through a particular pair of binoculars.

Oh Whistle and I'll Come to you, My Lad involves the ruins of a Knights Templar preceptory. In the story, this is in Monty's native Suffolk, probably Felixstowe.

But some of the best preserved and most mysterious Templar remains in the country are to be found at Garway.

For more than seven centuries, this order of medieval warrior monks has been gathering mystique like fairy dust. Established in the 12th century to protect Christian pilgrims, The Order of the Poor Knights of Christ and the Temple of Solomon got rich quick, having become the first international bankers and — allegedly — discovered lost treasures on the site of the famous temple in Jerusalem where they were based.

Were they the guardians of the Holy Grail? And what *was* the Holy Grail? According to the cult 1980s bestseller, *The Holy Blood and the Holy Grail*, later fictionalised in *The Da Vinci Code*, the Grail legends obscure the bloodline of Jesus and Mary Magdalene, who apparently were an item.

Or not. In *The Fabric of Sin*, I left all this alone and concentrated on the Templars themselves and, particularly, their last Grand Master, Jacques de Molay, who is said to have spent time in Garway.

You can read about all this in Audrey Tapper's *Knights Templar & Hospitaller in Herefordshire*, which collects all the known facts about Garway and the other local Templar sites, principally at Dinmore, so I'm not going to pinch Audrey's research here. Anyway, novels let you *develop* the facts.

The Church of St Michael
(Yes, another one)

Not much has actually changed in Garway since the Templar church was handed over to their successors, the Hospitallers. You can still see the remains of the circular nave, built in imitation of the Church of the Holy Sepulchre in Jerusalem. The sandstone tower, which seems to wear a kind of sardonic little smile and was originally separated from the body of the church, was also built by the Templars, whose stone coffin lids you'll find in window ledges and the chancel steps.

Templars everywhere. Still. And what exactly are those golden figures which appear in the picture I snapped when the red curtain was drawn across the nave (see page 13)?

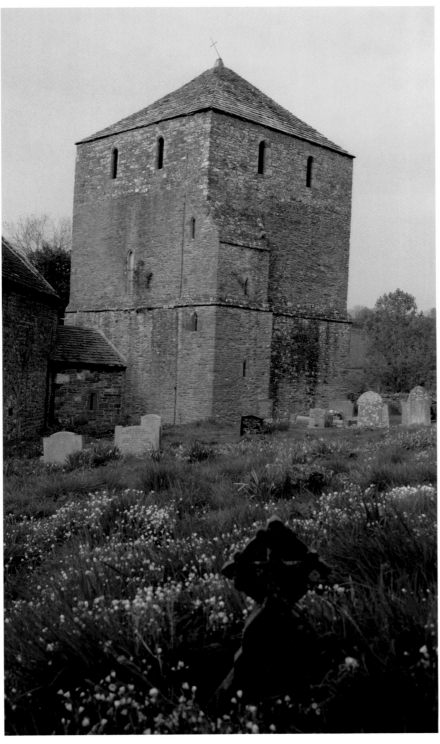

Garway Church is small, unspoiled but *never* cosy. An experienced dowser, exploring the interior with Sir Richard Heygate during research for Richard's book, with Philip Carr-Gomm, *English Magic*, in 2008, said he'd experienced a shattering sense of evil in the area of the piscina, once used to wash the communion chalice.

Personally, I've never detected evil here, but there's certainly a pervading air of secrecy. I was in the church one dappled autumn morning, with my wife, Carol, and local historian Sue Rice, when the dowser and Egyptologist John Ward perambulated the tower and suggested there was a secret room in which something had been kept. Outside, he arranged us all around a field where he'd dowsed the outline of a vanished building.

There's a lot still to be found here.

On the edge of farm buildings behind the church, the holy spring trickles, overhung by small, ribbony offerings — perhaps the water supply which first commended this place as a religious settlement.

Follow the stream to the edge of the churchyard, and there, among the farm buildings you can see the columbarium, like a kiln.

The dovecote. Probably built by the Templars and improved by the Hospitallers. One of the finest, best-preserved medieval dovecotes in Britain, its dove-chambers numbering an enigmatic 666. The Number of the Beast ... possibly. Nobody knows why it has this exact number of chambers, but the stone plinth in the middle is unlikely to be an altar to Satan.

This is where Merrily and Jane have that first fateful meeting with Mrs Morningwood, the alternative therapist and possibly one of the Nine Witches of Garway (we'll get to them).

Meanwhile, back in the church, on the left side of the chancel arch, you need to meet someone else.

Garway: The Holy Well (right)
and Columbarium (below)

Examples of the Green Man are found in churches all over Britain, with several in Herefordshire. A male face peers through twigs and leaves, teeth clenched around them. The *foliate face* is normally considered a pagan fertility symbol, but nobody really knows and nobody knows, either, why it's found in Christian churches.

Garway's Green Man however, is subtly different. As Sue Rice has pointed out, whatever is issuing from his mouth seems more like a cord with tassles than foliage ... and the cord is associated with Baphomet, the bearded head which the Knights Templar were said to have venerated and which was later turned into a scarily androgynous symbol sometimes connected with black magic.

The image of the Green Man filters through history and has royal connections. Charles II, peering through the branches of an oak tree while hiding from his enemies, is one example. The latest one, of course, is the Prince of Wales, champion of organic farming, energy conservation and alternative therapies, who may, apparently — given the problems encountered by the two previous King Charleses — decide to adopt another name on accession to the throne.

The Prince's business, The Duchy of Cornwall owns many thousands of acres in Herefordshire and acquired the Harewood Estate, only a few miles from Garway, where a working hamlet is being rebuilt, along with a large house.

The Harewood Estate also has a Knights Templar chapel.

It seemed reasonable that the Duchy, which owns many farms, should buy the Master House, so called because of its connection with Jacques de Molay, last Grand Master of the order.

De Molay was publicly burned in Paris after charges of heresy and borderline satanic worship were laid against the Templars by the King of France, Philip the Fair, and his friend the Pope. The basis of these charges seems to lie in the fact that the Templars were very rich and the King of France needed the money, but Baphomet doesn't seem to have been an invention of the prosecution and it's arguable that some Templar communities had become corrupted. My feeling is that de Molay himself, while a bit of an operator, was probably on the side of the angels. The climax of *The Fabric of Sin*, in which Jacques is remembered, occurs on the 700th aniversary of his death.

But let's return to M.R. James who, during a holiday in Herefordshire, went one day, with either Jane or Gwendolen or both of them, to visit Garway Church. A memorable visit, which he referred to later in a letter to Gwendolen:

> We must have offended somebody or something at Garway, I think. Probably we took it too much for granted, in speaking of it, that we should be able to do exactly as we pleased. Next time we shall know better. There is no doubt that it is a very rum place and needs careful handling.

Now, it could be that they simply left a gate open and were pursued by a farmer with a stick. And yet it's very much the sort of thing people say in an M.R. James ghost story. 'Somebody or something.' And it's the *place* that he describes as rum and in need of careful handling.

This figures.

M.R. James was often asked if he actually believed in ghosts and his careful reply was that he was prepared to consider the evidence.

In putting *Fabric* together, I looked at the plot of *Oh Whistle ...* which does involve an actual whistle, found by a visiting academic in the remains of those Knights Templar ruins in Suffolk. When he blows it he summons the wind ... and something else. Something made out of rumpled bedclothes, with a face of crumpled linen.

As recorded by Ella Mary Leather, whistling up the wind was once common practice amongst

Herefordshire farmers, to bring on a winnowing breeze. From Mrs Leather, too, I learned that Garway was one of the last places to maintain the *watch after death*, in which the whole household sat up all night when someone died on the premises. A pewter plate of salt was placed on the body, with a candle in its centre. I started to interweave these stories to seek out an explanation of Monty's reference to a *rum place*.

And it *is* a rum place. It did have four pubs, all linked to the heavens — the Sun, the Moon (the only one still open) the Globe and the Seven Stars.

And it did have that old saying,

There'll be nine witches from the bottom
of Orcop to the end of Garway Hill as
long as water flows ...

Candidates for the Nine are identified to this day.

11   The Uncoiling of the Serpent

The landscape itself was throwing off centuries like superfluous bedclothes, an old light pulsing to the surface, and Jane could feel the urgency of it in her spine.

To Dream of the Dead

Archaeologists are feeling this, too, in the wake of the finding of The Dinedor Serpent, or The Rotherwas Ribbon as it was orginally and more prosaically called by local councillors who were wishing it would just curl up and die.

The subplot of *The Remains of an Altar* involved the discovery of ancient stones under a site in Coleman's Meadow, Ledwardine which Herefordshire Council had earmarked for development. In the book, this led to major protests, involving environmental, heritage and pagan factions, led, of course, by Jane Watkins.

Even as that book was being prepared for publication, archaeologists were uncovering what was described as a unique Bronze Age ritual construction ... right in the path of a new road planned by that same local authority.

It was almost uncanny, and there was no way I could get out of using the Dinedor Serpent in a future novel. Especially as it, too, generated a massive row, with the council accused of — literally — a cover-up in its determination to make sure the road went through.

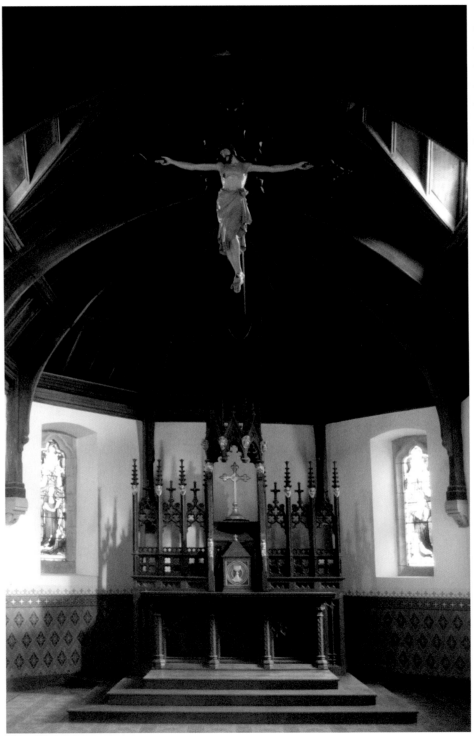

A man chained himself to a JCB and eight people were arrested for aggravated trespass for refusing to leave the council's HQ, where the issue was to be discussed in private. Because there weren't enough spare cells at Hereford, some of them were taken to Worcester, where they languished for hours. 'I spent the time psychically cleansing my cell,' one woman said.

In the end, all charges were dropped, but it left a nasty taste.

Rotherwas has not, in recent years, been the most favoured part of Hereford. Industrial estates — and Rotherwas has Hereford's biggest — are seldom scenic. The area's architectural jewel, Rotherwas Chapel, Elizabethan family chapel of the Catholic Bodenhams, is just round the corner from the public dump.

But the chapel, the dump and the factories all share the city's finest backdrop: Dinedor Hill, with its woodland and its Celtic camp.

And now the Dinedor Serpent, which the Council has always preferred to refer to as the Rotherwas Ribbon — far less sexy; who would ever want to visit that?

The Serpent

So ... what exactly is it, and why was it constructed?

Well, of course, we don't know.

It was found during a routine archaeological scan of the proposed site of the Rotherwas relief road — a planned shortcut out of the industrial estate.

There never was, to be honest, much to see.

In *To Dream of the Dead*, a councillor dismisses the Serpent as 'patio gravel'. Which, as you can see in the picture above (part of the Serpent is exposed behind me and the dowser Chris Hinsley — he's the one with the beard) is not entirely insulting.

The small stones are believed to be fire-cracked, the result of rocks dropped into a burning pit. The original theory was that they were then used for the surface of a path, some kind of ritual walkway possibly all the way from the top of Dinedor Hill to the River Wye. But the fact that there was no substructure suggested they weren't exactly for walking on.

Could they simply have been chippings thrown away after the stones had been used for some other purpose — the first industrial waste to be dumped at Rotherwas? But why were so many of the fragments found to be quartz?

Archaeologists began to consider the idea that because of the quartz content, likely to glow in the moonlight, the curving path could have been intended as some kind of Bronze Age special-effect, reflecting the meandering of the river. Awesome under a full moon.

Somehow, it answers all the criteria for an authentic spirit path, connecting the sacred river (rivers were seen as entrances to the otherworld) with Hereford's holy hill. Unsuitable for human beings, a point of access for the ancestors.

If it is a monument, the only comparable ones are the Serpent Mounds of Ohio, conserved at huge expense. As an American said, on hearing about Dinedor, 'We'd kill to have a find like that.'

In *To Dream of the Dead*, someone *is* killed, part of him displayed on the preaching cross near the ruins of the Blackfriars Monastery, which crouch behind the medieval Coningsby Hospital in Widemarsh Street.

In some cities the Blackfriars Monastery would be a major tourist attraction. In Hereford it's a secret. Wander in there, the chances are you'll be on your own. But at least it's conserved.

The future of the Serpent remains unclear. The road is now open. Archaeologists tended to agree that the only way of preserving the remains was to cover them up, but the bitter irony of having industrial traffic roaring over a possible ritual path has not gone unnoticed.

The day before *To Dream of the Dead* was published, the *Hereford Journal* published a reader's letter as a page lead under the headline

Look out for the curse
of the Dinedor Serpent

The letter more or less suggested that Hereford Council, by going ahead with the road out of Rotherwas, had opened up its own fast-track to hell ...

For many local people, the idea of hell is what the Council might have in mind for the green countryside now opened up by the road.

In *To Dream*, the parallels between the Serpent and the Coleman's Meadow excavation are underlined again.

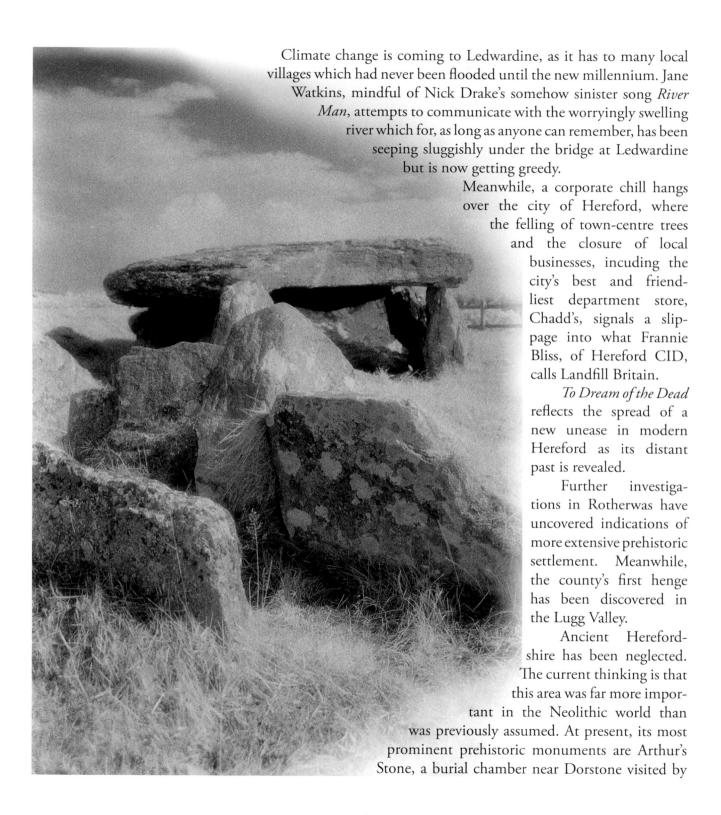

Climate change is coming to Ledwardine, as it has to many local villages which had never been flooded until the new millennium. Jane Watkins, mindful of Nick Drake's somehow sinister song *River Man*, attempts to communicate with the worryingly swelling river which for, as long as anyone can remember, has been seeping sluggishly under the bridge at Ledwardine but is now getting greedy.

Meanwhile, a corporate chill hangs over the city of Hereford, where the felling of town-centre trees and the closure of local businesses, incuding the city's best and friendliest department store, Chadd's, signals a slippage into what Frannie Bliss, of Hereford CID, calls Landfill Britain.

To Dream of the Dead reflects the spread of a new unease in modern Hereford as its distant past is revealed.

Further investigations in Rotherwas have uncovered indications of more extensive prehistoric settlement. Meanwhile, the county's first henge has been discovered in the Lugg Valley.

Ancient Herefordshire has been neglected. The current thinking is that this area was far more important in the Neolithic world than was previously assumed. At present, its most prominent prehistoric monuments are Arthur's Stone, a burial chamber near Dorstone visited by

Jane and her boyfriend Eirion in *The Remains of an Altar*, the Queen Stone in the Wye Valley and the Wern Derys standing stone, near Michaelchurch Escley, pictured on the cover of *To Dream of the Dead*.

The title of which comes from an old saying noted by Ella Mary Leather in *The Folklore of Herefordshire*:

To Dream of the Dead is a sign of rain.

How would anyone come up with a saying like that?

Only on the Border ...

List of Photographs

The Merrily Watkins series (so far) with principal locations

The Wine of Angels	Ledwardine
Midwinter of the Spirit	Hereford
A Crown of Lights	The Radnor Valley
The Cure of Souls	The Frome Valley
The Lamp of the Wicked	Ross-on-Wye and the Forest of Dean
The Prayer of the Night Shepherd	Kington
The Smile of a Ghost	Ludlow
The Remains of an Altar	The Malverns
The Fabric of Sin	Garway
To Dream of the Dead	Ledwardine, Hereford

Also available is the CD, *Songs from Lucy's Cottage*, by Lol Robinson with Hazey Jane II

Select Bibliography

Mark Bowden, with David Field & Helen Winton, *The Malvern Hills, An ancient landscape* (English Heritage)

Paul Broadhurst, *The Green Man and the Dragon* (Mythos)

Bromyard and District Local History Society, *A Pocketful of Hops*

Ronald Bryer, *Not the Least, The Story of Little Malvern* (The Self-publishing Association)

Brian Cave, *The Countryside around Weston and Lea* (The Forest Bookshop)

Michael Cox, *M.R. James, An Informal Portrait* (Oxford)
   (Also strongly recommended: *The Ghosts and Scholars* magazine and online, edited by Rosemary Pardoe)

Paul Devereux, *Spirit Roads* (Collins & Brown)
               Haunted Land (Piatkus)

Pat Hughes and Heather Hurley, *The Story of Ross* (Logaston Press)

Michael Kennedy, *The Life of Elgar* (Cambridge)
   (Also well worth getting hold of Ken Russell's early BBC documentary on Elgar)

Ella Mary Leather, *The Folklore of Herefordshire* (Lapridge; currently out of print)

Patrick Jasper Lee, *We Borrow the Earth* (Thorsons)

David Lloyd, *The Concise History of Ludlow* (Merlin Unwin)

John Michell, *The View over Atlantis* (Garnstone, Abacus)
              The New View over Atlantis (Thames & Hudson)
              City of Revelation (Abacus)

Jerrold Northrop Moore, *Elgar, Child of Dreams* (Faber)

Roy Palmer, *Herefordshire Folklore* (Logaston Press)
            The Folklore of Radnorshire (Logaston Press)
            The Folklore of (old) Monmouthshire (Logaston Press)

Ron Shoesmith, *Alfred Watkins — a Herefordshire Man* (Logaston Press; out of print)

Ron Shoesmith and Andy Johnson (editors) *Ludlow Castle* (Logaston Press)

Fred Slater, *The Nature of Central Wales* (Barracuda)

Audrey Tapper, *Knights Templar and Hospitaller in Herefordshire* (Logaston Press)

Thomas Traherne, *Selected Poems and Prose* ed. Alan Bradford (Penguin)

Joan and Brian Thomas (and others) *Garway Hill Through the Ages* (Logaston Press)

Alfred Watkins, *The Old Straight Track*